What people are saying about Big Murphy's

"Nathan Minnehan, founder of Big Murphy's clothing, is a unique individual, unlike anyone I've ever met.
Among many things, Nathan is a HUMAN BRANDER.
Entrepreneurs spend thousands of dollars branding products. Nathan brands people.
I am one of them. I've done a lot in my life.
Nathan takes all that you've done and spreads it out on the kitchen table, then assembles it all into a memorable and profitable brand, separating you from who you were, to who you should be.
He encouraged me to write my book successfully, and together, we are creating an empire I didn't know I had within me.
-Jerry Lobozzo
Author of -SPEAK FOR YOURSELF
7 Powerful Ways to SPEAK UP. SHUT UP. and SHOW UP.

There's buying clothing and leather goods, then there's working with Big Murphy's. The experience with Nathan and his representatives transcends expectations and moves into a relationship that you can tell is special from minute one. Both suits that I've co-designed with Nathan are exceptional and my go-to garments for making an impression. I can't seem to walk into a room without exuding the perfect presence. Thanks in large part to Big Murphy's. That being said, I needed something to convey my sense of the world on a multi-use and everyday level. For this task, Nathan made me a stellar leather carrying case for my MacBook. It's a light brown leather, with red pig skin interior, monogrammed and set off by that big spirited Big Murphy's face embossed on it. A subtle head turner at every meeting.
Be a member of society on your own terms, be Big Murphy's.
Dario Lobozzo Strategic Accounts Director, Security Matters

Nathan's work has far exceeded my expectations at every turn. I first met him in one of my networking groups, and I was immediately captivated by his energy and positivity. I am an attorney and wear suits regularly. Nathan clearly knew what he was doing and gave great recommendations. He came to my office and measured me up for my first fitted gray suit. The suit was ready sooner than I anticipated,, and Nathan was quick to make corrections in the pant and shirt sizes for me. I wear my Big Murphy's gray suit at least twice a week now. It feels and looks great. I was so pleased with the result, I asked Nathan to make me my tuxedo for my upcoming wedding. I am equally as pleased with the result. He went through every detail meticulously to make sure I received exactly what I was looking for. I highly recommend Nathan to anyone looking for the perfect suit. As a bonus, Nathan will impart some words of positivity and wisdom during every session...at least he did with me. Thanks Nathan! Already looking forward to my next suit!
Haig A. Himidian
Associate Attorney at Taxman, Pollock, Murray & Bekkerman, LLC

5 STARS-After getting a custom suit by Nathan, I have received more compliments and comments than anything I have ever worn. I know I am going to look sharp and feel great when I put on this custom jacket. I wear it all the time now!
Joel Schaub
Vice President of Mortgage Lending at Guaranteed Rate

I was introduced to Nathan through a mutual friend as a fashion consultant and maker of custom clothes. We designed a custom blazer together. He presented options and gave suggestions, and also worked with me to design something I was super into. The result was a fun experience and a beautiful blazer that fits to perfection. I honestly feel

like I'm driving a Ferrari when I wear it.
Ben Daugherty
Senior Consultant - HCM, Advanced Compensation and Report Writing at TopBloc

Nathan has an incredible sense for not only style but making sure each person's individual style comes out. Rather than placing his clients into a box as some custom clothiers attempt to do Nathan will construct a brand new box for you made specifically to your recommendations, ideals and vision. When looking to bring your business to the next level the right clothes should be one of the first places to look and for this need one need look no further than Nathan Minnehan.
Matthew Peebles
Owner and Principal Consultant, Enrollment Specialists, LLC

Your Health and Life Insurance Superhero
Nathan created a work of art for me that I wear whenever I want to be the instant center of attention, and/ or make a profoundly impactful positive first impression in business meetings. I am, by nature, a very confident person. But having this fabulous suit is like turbo charging what I already have to ridiculous levels. Your clothes tell your story. Let Nathan's fabulous suits tell yours." If you have any questions, email me. therealrj77@gmail.com www.rjcoaching.com
Ross Jeffries
CEO, Head Trainer at Subtle Words That Sell

"Nothing makes me feel as good as my Big Murphy's jackets. Nathan knows how to bring your game to the next level. Buy his clothes, see how you feel, and watch what happens."
Greg Reid, San Diego-based author (65 books) and motivation speaker known for "Three Feet from Gold," A Napoleon Hill Foundation Bestseller.

"Packing for my speaking gigs has become a stress-free, fun experience as I simply place my Big Murphy's jackets inside of my suitcase, and take them out wrinkle free upon arrival. The fabric and craftsmanship is impeccable."
The Creator and A Founder of the Make-A-Wish Foundation

"I'm pleased to announce I obtained $750,000 of justice for my client this week at trial. Her father was run over and killed by a taxi in NYC as he was riding his motorcycle in September 2012. The jury found the taxi 100% liable for causing the crash and that the decedent was conscious and suffered for one minute before he died."
"Have to give a big shout out to my friend Nathan Minnehan whose custom made suits and shirts kept me looking great and gave me the confidence to defeat an attorney who was the named partner at the defense firm, and had thirty years and hundreds of trials of more experience than me!"
Elliot Dolby-Shields, Criminal Justice Attorney

"Nathan even got Tony Robbins to say, 'I look fresh.'"
Manny Lopez, Los Angeles-based tech entrepreneur.

"Shirts are dope. As a big man, it's hard to find ones that fit, and these rock!"
Luke Gelman, Commercial Real Estate Broker

MENSWEAR REVOLUTION

MENSWEAR REVOLUTION

THE SECRET LIFE OF A CLOTHIER

NATHAN MINNEHAN

MENSWEAR REVOLUTION
THE SECRET LIFE OF A CLOTHIER

By Nathan Minnehan

ISBN: 979-8-950444-02-9

Published by: Inspiration On Tap, LLC
2336 SE Ocean Blvd #222
Stuart, FL 34996

TABLE OF CONTENTS

Part 2 - Box Pressed

The best cloth may come from Europe, but the best suits are not made in Italy
Why the Iberian Peninsula will always be the best at one thing
Why a nice set of tits and a world-class car collection can sell $10,000 suits
Pro athletes PAY, but do you really need them to create a TOP suit business

Part 3 -Maduro

Why your local suit company is ripping everyone off and how you stand to profit
Why the New York Knicks clothier got fired, and why you could replace him
Why every guy knows a guy and how to become that guy
Getting paid and getting laid have two things in common

Part 4 -Churchill

Why it is ok to never grow up and get a real job
How to be a lion in a world of lambs
Instagram is for time suckers, but we still watch the reels
Real men don't care, but real men will never tell you that
The secret revealed

The End

DRESS ITALIAN, DRIVE GERMAN, KISS HOWEVER, AND GET PAID THE BIG BUCKS TO DO IT!

BONUS CONTENT

CLOTHES MORE DEALS
THE ART OF FRAMING POSSIBILITY

Preface

I can remember sitting in my car, pulled over in Chicago's Gold Coast. Behind on my car payments. Struggling to make this business work. Toiling and struggling to understand the custom suit and garment business.
It was then that I made the decision to make it work. To burn all of the ships, and figure it out.

Suffering the pains of countless remakes, mismeasuring, and constantly making it up to clients either on delivery times or fit, I decided to never give up. To embrace those setbacks as lessons, and grist for the mill in creating the foundation to my future success as a well-known custom clothier.

While I have been blessed to serve clients like best-selling author and filmmaker Dr. Greg Reid, founder of the Make-A-Wish Foundation Frank Shankwitz, and Ron Klein, inventor of the magnetic strip on the credit card, I didn't find them by accident. Refusing to give up, I persevered. I refused to quit and chose instead to be humble and trust the process. I followed the signs and synchronicities that success will show you along your journey; sleeping in my car, on clients' and friend's couches, at random and not random people's houses, in my 47,000-mile journey across the country selling suits in 2019.

Believe it or not, I did that trek during the course of seven months.
But to become a master of the suit business requires not just selling suits and clothing, but also delivering great clothes. That is what separates the best from the rest. This subtle distinction is the difference between one-off sales and repeat clients that become friends, pals, and family for life.

If you want to create an amazing life, and make your business an art of living and loving what you do, all while creating amazing connections along the way, then the custom suit business could be for you.

But do not be fooled. Like everything that's worth anything, it takes focus, discipline, and a no-quit mindset to do it. The good news is you've found the only portal I know in existence capable or even willing to bring you up to speed on a very secretive trade whose secrets no one reveals.

You might ask why I'm doing this?

Well, let's say it's a combination of wanting and needing to pay it forward.
In 2020 my life changed. By virtue of connections I had created in my journey as a clothier, I acted quickly, set up a mask business, and a financial miracle happened in my life. I bought my dream home in Portugal and was reunited with the love of my life.

I spent many months happy, but the joy of the windfall began to fade. I realized that the only real and sustaining joy in life is to create and affect impact in the world. To find a way to wholeheartedly pay it forward and never look back.

It was then that I began to realize that through my journey of hard knocks I had been bestowed with one of the most awesome sets of business knowledge in the world of gentlemen enterprises. You see, during my years of mastering my process as a clothier and building my suit business, I saw one transformation after the other. The clothing I was making for my clients wasn't just boosting their confidence, it was changing their lives.

I saw mice become men. Shy guys into sly guys. Potential into power. And single into happily married. While this all may sound quite romantic, and fun, and you probably think I'm exaggerating, why don't you take a look at some of the testimonials at the beginning of the book? I have clients that claim the clothing I built for them has literally won trials with

multi-million dollar verdicts.
Think that's all? Think again! Clothing has the power to frame possibility and attract the pivotal success moments you desire to bring your dream world into existence. As they say "if you build it, they will come," well, the saying rings true with clothing as well. Change the clothing, change the man. Build the clothing, build the man. And that's just the tip of the iceberg!

To illustrate how important the philosophy of clothing is to this entire Menswear Revolution, I am including my book CLOTHES MORE DEALS here in the back of this book.

May these two texts guide you as I was guided. And when you are ready to take action, and receive your greatness, I will be waiting for you at MenswearRevolution.com. And to prove it I'm going to even give you my personal phone number, so when you're ready, I'll always be just a phone call away. Here goes, (+1 585 703-4506). That's my real number, and this book and my course are the real deal. Want to see for yourself? Go to MENSWEARREVOLUTION.COM and download my free course **Instant Style,** and begin making the pivotal clothing mindset switch today!

Foreword

"A dream written down with a date becomes a goal. A goal broken down into steps becomes a plan. A plan backed by action makes your dreams come true."

- Dr. Greg Reid

It's funny, I remember when Nathan Minnehan first popped up on my Facebook feed with a wooden bicycle he was peddling from Portugal. And then custom eyewear, leather notebooks, and leather bags. I thought, here's a cool cat, I'm going to make him an offer and see what he's made of.

I called him up and said, "Listen, kid, I don't have much time, but if you donate one of those groovy $5,000 wooden bicycles to my conference charity auction, I'll give you a chance to speak on stage and it'll change your life forever."

Nathan said yes, took action to make it happen, and drove 2500 miles across the country with the wooden bike in his car to personally transport and deliver it himself.

I don't know about you, but in my book, that spells

commitment.

You see, a long time ago when I wanted to become a successful author I was led through a series of connected circumstances to interview the world's contemporary millionaires and billionaires. That journey took required action and commitment to make it happen. It really is the action in the 'law of attraction' that makes your dreams come true.

So, look, this book is a golden opportunity staring you in the face. It's an opportunity to what I call "get paid to do what you're already going to do."

You like nice clothes right? You can appreciate the difference between a bespoke custom suit and one that's off the rack, right?

Well, aren't you going to buy and wear custom suits anyway? Why not learn from Nathan and seize this unique golden opportunity that he is offering through the Menswear Revolution masterclass?

The answer is simple. Make the investment, do the work, and reap the benefits.

Look good. Do good. Feel good. Be good.

Now take the tip from my bestseller, Wealth Made Easy, and get the wealth hack by connecting the dots, and go ahead and get paid to do what you're already going to do.

You got this. Now go, be a champion, and take your life to the next level!

-Dr. Greg Reid
Author, Speaker, Filmmaker
Gregreid.com

Introduction

"Here's to life and ain't it grand. I just got a divorce from my old man. And here's to the judge and his grand old decision. He gave the kids to my husband and they ain't even his'n."

\- *Mimi*

I can still hear these words echoing in my head from years ago when I first heard them sung through the laughing crying voice of my Mimi (my grandmother). Among her many phrases, this was one that really stuck. It seems that the wisdom of the generations can be boiled down to a few quirky lines like that. Ones that so often seem to reach out and shake us, grasping at what can too often not be spoken publicly, and what few have the balls to even admit privately.

Let's face it, as a society we're fucked. We've been duped. Duped into jobs, marriages, and lives that we discover long after are things we've been sold into. Like a brand new car with a high-interest rate, hanging over our heads month after month until it's finally paid off. Only to discover it's not worth shit. And in fact, someone else was banking on our blindspot the whole way, laughing all the way to the bank.

Are you confused about what I'm even talking about here? Good. You thought this is a book about clothing. You're wrong. This is a book about life. First, we have to call a spade a spade before we can play our best hand if you get my drift, so let's get back to it.
You see, we're all after one thing, and one thing only. Success. We say that everyone is entitled to their own definition of it, yet we're sold success every single day on all the social media platforms, billboards, commercials, and in all of the subtle nuances of conversations and who's who. And my friend's 'this', and my friend's 'that'. It's all marketing marinated in who's got MONEY. Whoever has the most money wins, right? Bigger house, nicer car, hotter wife, better clothes, better schools for our kids. Better food, better health care, and in general, better options, right?

So, if that's what success really is then why don't we all just say it, and go do whatever it takes to get as much money as possible, so we can go out there and make all of the upgrades? Right? Go get a bigger house, maybe find a hotter wife, upgrade our wheels, better schools for the kids, better clothes, better watch, better food, better everything. Isn't that the goal?

I mean, that's success, right? We're sold these ideas everyday, are we not?

Well, let's skip the mumbo jumbo and pull back the curtain

on life's pending reality check that's coming whether you like it or not. You're going to die one day. You and everyone else that you know. That's the reality. Now, while you're technically still alive you're going to find out that somewhere along the way, the way you feel about the life you've created is going to be more important to you than what you have in fact created.

Put it this way. Someone could sign over a check for 10 million dollars to you tomorrow. You could then cash that check and go out and buy everything you need to live a rich life. Just like on Instagram and Pinterest. Then you could kick back and enjoy your life, right?

WRONG. WRONG. WRONG. WRONG.

That's a road leading to emptiness. Now, suppose instead that you create 10 million dollars through a process. One in which you learn lessons along the way and deploy those dollars to build the life you're dreaming of along the way, then you'd find yourself in a much different place. It does matter how you get to where you're going. AND THAT is why it's important to decide your path from the beginning. Why it's important not to skip any steps.

There is a reason they're called stepping stones. When you skip the stepping stones, you may risk falling in the water, and the water can be treacherous. So is the road to real success.

There are no shortcuts. And if you try to cheat success, success will cheat you. You'll wake up like so many people as they get old in life, feeling empty. Wondering what it was all for.

Now, there is a solution to this disease in our society. This emptiness which plagues so many. And while it may seem relatively simple, its application is absolutely profound.

In order to be successful and to become a success, we must first understand that success is a fabric. And the fabric of success must first be woven before it can be CMT'd (cut-measured-trimmed) into one's personal reality.

What does that even mean?

Well, I'm talking about the ups and downs. The number of times you got knocked down and how quickly you got back up, only to get knocked back down again. Over and over until someone said, "What the hell is wrong with you, are you nuts? Get a real job!" Or, "That's never going to work!" But you kept on going. You stared fear in its bloody, devilish face of darkness and showed the light of perseverance right into the void until suddenly almost magically you found yourself walking along a city sidewalk on a bright sunny day living on your clock, and not someone else's. With money in the bank, gas in the tank, a house all paid, and your life suddenly "made", you stop for a moment and realize, "I did it." Isn't that what we all want?

To have that feeling?
Well, that sickening pattern of failures and tiny successes… That up and down hem and haw… That inconsistent pace of challenges and triumphs… The extent to which you are willing to subject yourself to life's grimmest, darkest, meanest sides, is directly correlated to the finesse of the fabric of success that you will one day be shrouded in.

In the world of custom suiting, the prestige of each suit fabric is measured in microns and commonly referred to as "supers." Super 100s, Super 110's, 120's, 130's, 140's, 150's, 160's, etc. Before a fabric is woven, a diameter of thread is selected. The finer the thread, the softer the fabric, the higher the prestige.

The same goes for success. Those who are willing to, in Shakespeare's words, "suffer the slings and arrows of misfortune…" "To be or not to be…" a success. Those are the ones whose prestige of success will be determined by the mightiness of their character. Their willingness to get back up when they have been slammed to the ground, beaten to a pulp by life's misfortunes, until like magic, all of life's misfortunes one day turn into a sort of philosopher's stone.

A stone so powerful that just one tiny shard can mint a heap of raw material into pure gold.
That is alchemy. And for those who want to play on life's

highest levels of success and satisfaction, they have to first know, feel, and discover the power of these truths firsthand for themselves.

That is why you cannot gift success to someone, or become more successful by hoarding anything. The most successful people in the world are those willing to give their best stuff away in service of those who dare to follow their talents to the dark places they most certainly lead.

That is the opportunity for success. And that is how one becomes more successful. So, here we are. Two strangers on a page, about to go on a journey. One that requires absolute trust, for both you the reader, and I the writer, are never to be the same once this journey concludes. For it will most certainly preclude the commencement of a much larger journey ahead.

So, let's not delay. Fortune favors the bold, and only the bold will have the courage to stay the course, fight in the darkness, and rise and rise again until lambs become lions.

To victory. To success. To the alchemy, mystery, and to the upholding of its sacred code of process. Without it, there is no progress.

Preamble

IV

Chess Not Checkers

"What we do in life echoes in eternity"

- *Gladiator*

Ever wondered if things that rhyme in language rhyme on a deeper level as well? How about chess and success?

Chess is a strategic game in which the one with the most clever strategy to capture the king wins. Have you ever considered or pondered the wisdom locked inside of this ancient game?

The legend goes that chess (or a similar game that eventually became chess) was invented by monks in the 6th century in India. The emperor had ordered the monks to create a game to indirectly educate the people and inject them with vital wisdom. To think that this ancient game is still the most prestigious intellectual sport to date is quite impressive. What's more, is its contemporary flare. We saw the status of its modern popularity in The Queens Gambit, a recent Netflix series where a young girl breaks out of foster care and poverty, pulling herself up by her bootstraps all through the tactful mastery of the age-old game.

What if chess could give us a few clues about success and how to attain it? Does its rhyming relationship have a deeper connection? Let's think...

The short answer is yes. There is a reason why people say "chess not checkers." It implies strategy, and if you're going to succeed in life, and do it faster than you are currently, then a solid strategy is key to getting ahead.

Can you get more successful? Well, the answer surely is yes. But how can you be more successful? You earn and gain influence. And the fastest, simplest way to do that is to present yourself in such a way that people notice when you arrive.

Show Up Powerfully to Close Effortlessly

In sales or life, we are always closing. Whether it's merely gaining the unspoken confidence of those around you or naturally commanding those around you to acquiesce gladly and willingly without lifting a finger.

Ever notice how people's moods change when a sharply dressed person walks through the door? How the energy of the room changes, and people all around suddenly turn and notice. Maybe they even flash a smile. That person that just walked in earned instant credibility. And in the modern world, instant credibility is one step closer to instant trust, and trust is the most valuable currency on the planet.

Six months ago I was at a conference. I brought a few of my favorite suits and prepared to be myself, go out there, and have fun meeting people.

One day into the three day personal development conference I had about ten people raving about my suit and asking for my contact. On the second day I was measuring someone at lunch, then after dinner, and then again at midnight next to the bar in the hotel. The following day I had five fittings one after the other in between speakers, lunch, dinner and the evening gala. Truth be told, I met a guy at one o'clock in the morning. He said, "Hey I need a suit like that one!"

"You got it", I told him. "Let's measure you up right now."
"Great," he said, "let's do it!"

I literally met him at one in the morning, measured him around 1:45-2:10 AM, took payment by credit card processor on my phone and headed up to bed.

Eight weeks later he got his suit, and sent me a photo of him and his entire real estate team together in his new suit. He looked, AMAZING. What a transformation. I was so impressed. Honestly it still amazes me how powerful the transformation is that occurs when I make people these garments. And in many cases, it is literally life-changing. And guess what? New found confidence equals new found personal power, and personal power drives success!

So, how did being a clothier help me to succeed here?

Well, not only did I absorb the wisdom and knowledge of some of the smartest and most successful millionaires and billionaires on the planet, I got paid to do it!

Not only did I gain literally a dozen new clients, I also made a dozen new friends.

And guess what, now they know a guy who makes suits, and does a great job, so naturally the referrals and repeat business just keeps on coming. And that is why it's so important to show up powerfully, and truly curate your personal style and personal brand to harness and leverage the energy around you every day and especially at key moments like this one.

V

BACK DOOR TO SUCCESS

"You feel better in a new suit rather than an old one. The old suit is filled with your old thought. For thought is a substance that attaches itself and permeates whichever is nearest to he who thinks. Your old suit is filled more or less with the depressed evil or immature states of mind you have experienced in wearing it. When you put it on, you are putting on more or less of such low and despondent thought."

-Prentice Mulfort, *Thoughts Are Things*

Have you ever noticed how putting on a new suit or special garment gives you almost certain and sudden power? A new sense of self and possibility? Well, that's because it does! Clothing is the one thing that, like acupuncture, touches the tiniest yet most poignant parts of ourselves, and magically transforms one's energy.

Ever tried on one of your old garments while going through old clothes that were challenging to let go of and donate? Ever notice that nostalgia and attachment? For a moment it's romantic and endearing... maybe it even sparks some memories. But deep down you know you can't wear that article of clothing any longer and truly be at your best.

Imagine you were preparing for an important interview or date. Wouldn't you want to feel your absolute best? It's obvious that you'd want a go-to garment to execute on those kinds of key days. You wouldn't wear your grandfather's old suit to a job interview if you have a brand new one in the closet waiting to be worn and uplift you to your higher self, right? And why is that? Well, as Prentice Mulford says in his age-old classic Thoughts are Things, an old suit carries with it old thoughts and older less powerful versions of ourselves. The key is to create at higher levels of vibration and heal whatever is holding us back from the past. To do that we must be willing to bravely give up the old to embrace the new.

I recently revisited the words of Dr. Maxwell Maltz in his book Psycho-Cybernetics and recalled the profound ways that he had framed such subtleties. In his work, he talks a lot about transformations of one's personality by transforming some outer insecurity the person has. He states:

"If personality had a face... this non physical face of personality seems to be the real key to personality change. If it remains scarred, stained, distorted, or inferior, the person himself acts out this role in his behavior, regardless of the changes in physical appearance. If this face of personality could be reconstructed, if old emotional scars could be removed, then the person himself changes. When I began to explore this area, I found more and more phenomena that confirmed the fact that the self image, the individual's mental, physical, and spiritual concept or picture of himself is the real key to personality and behavior."

Isn't that amazing? As I was stating in the preface of this text, I have literally witnessed one transformation after the other when it comes to building clothing for my clients. One of my favorite types of new clients is someone who has never had a custom suit or shirt made for them before. The glow and smile that instantly comes over them when they try it on is so satisfying, I can barely put it into words. Once they receive their new garments, the real magic happens, and they begin to vibrate on a higher level and start attracting success almost effortlessly.

A lot of my clients are lawyers. They work very hard, and like to dress nice. The day their new suits come in is like Christmas! You can see the excitement come over them as they look over their garments with deep satisfaction. And in that moment, it is then that I know and they know, they are staring at their new next level.

If there were a back door to success it would be as simple as getting rid of all of the old garments that don't serve you. Garments that make you feel small and insignificant, and remind you of past failures. To discard them all. Then, find a person, a phenomenal clothier like myself, or in the case of this book, become one. (To learn more about becoming a custom clothier, go to: MENSWEARREVOLUTION.COM)

VI

REVERSE ENGINEERING SUCCESS THROUGH SUIT FREQUENCY

"Match the frequency of the reality you want and you cannot help but get that reality. It can be no other way. This is not philosophy. This is physics."

-Darryl Anka

The usual relationship between success and custom clothing is to earn your way up the social ladder until you're able to afford to wear custom clothing. For most people it's something that they begin to become interested in once they've reached a certain level of achievement. We're told not to stand out too much. To not look "too good" until you have the pockets to back it up. But I'm not talking about renting Lamborghinis here and posing on Instagram as a heavy-hitter. I'm talking about changing our perception about the cost of clothing. For instance, a guy shopping at Men's Wearhouse and buying a "custom made to measure" suit for $400, compared to a guy stepping it up, and investing in a $1200-$1500 suit. The first guy can buy three for the price of the second guy's suit, but can any of those three suits elevate his energetic frequency to the subtle and secret heights of the completely custom suit the guy is receiving in the $1200-$1500 price range? Not a chance. The cut, fabric, and detail of a truly custom suit when mixed with the character of an individual striving forward to be their best possible version is like adding nitroglycerin to their success. But more on those specific details later in this book.

In general, the common narrative in society is that only those who have truly earned a certain level of success are worthy of wearing such garments and anyone else is really just posing.

But what if you could reverse engineer success through clothing? What if you could change the frequency you operate on by wearing the highest frequency clothing that exists? What if your closet could become a key support to unlocking and unleashing your greatness to a set of consistent feelings of high vibration that, worn and experienced daily, day after day, would have no choice but to mold you into an individual who consistently operates on his highest frequencies?

Do you know that on weekends I tend to wear jeans, a black t-shirt, and a blazer? Do you know why? I need to recharge. My mindset is so sharp and tuned at all hours of the day every day of the week by virtue of wearing such high-frequency clothing that I really need a day or two to reset and experience some intentional lethargy. The opposite is true during the week. Come Monday morning I am putting my wheels in motion and intuitively choosing which suit, shirt, and tie to wear that day. As soon as I begin my morning dressing routine I can feel my higher frequency engaging. Down to the cologne and particular essential oil I add a drop of for increased mental focus, I'm like a turbojet taxing on the runway, before taking off at supersonic speed.

In my day-to-day, my activities range from design tasks to customer interaction, but primarily these days it's focused around a few key areas in the trading day, and the rest of my work fits nicely in between. The level of intense focus that I experience during my days is quite high and often engaged for several hours on end. I engage at this level and so my garments need to be able to hold my vibration in these important moments where every millisecond counts big time $$$.

As far as I'm concerned, whether you work in finance, real estate, sales, tech, or whatever, your vibration is everything. The studies are out there. Frequency creates reality. And if you're going to be a high performer you have to learn how to hack into your highest frequency and stay there. That is the key. Now, what are the constants in our daily lives? Who, what, where, when. "Who" starts with you. "What" pertains to what you allow, disallow, or intentionally create, carry or put on. "Where" is your environment, and you better believe it shapes your reality. "When" is time, and time is constant; never stops. So, in all of this, what "thing" can you really physically control that you can ensure will always be a variable that you are in charge of in the ever-changing landscape of our daily lives? That's right, you guessed it. It's our clothing. It's what we wear and what we carry. The question is... Is what you're wearing and carrying with you connecting you with a higher frequency or a lower frequency? Are you being naturally projected into your highest self, or dragged down and feeling "off?"

Now, the cost of the garments aside. There are certain garments that have the power to lift you up, and others that have the power to tear you down. Well orchestrated, a wardrobe could give you the power to convert and connect effortlessly across every aspect of life. If you intentionally build your wardrobe and your garments, you are in fact becoming the architect of future powerful and life-changing moments that are currently open opportunities on life's horizon.

The question becomes, what is it really costing you to not build your garments and your wardrobe with this powerful knowledge in mind? What leverage are you currently missing and opportunities are you currently passing on all because you're not daily tuning effortlessly into your higher frequency? As we know, left to chance, few things will become consistent. But when pre-imagined, created, and built to perfection, almost anything is possible. Just look at the magnificent architectural structures around us, notice people's attraction to them. Now, what if that could be you? What if just by dressing with that level of intention, you yourself could be walking daily and effortlessly to your highest level of life and success. Your higher self lives on a frequency and the only way to access it is to feel and enter that frequency daily and effortlessly. And what I know for sure is that we all must put on clothes to walk outside. The question is, are your clothes an investment or a liability to your success?

VII

FEEL LIKE A MILLION TO ATTRACT MILLIONS

"Definiteness of purpose is the starting point of all achievement"

-W. Clement Stone

Where does all great wealth truly begin? Is it just like magic that suddenly out of nowhere one's bank account balance jumps from one thousand to one million dollars overnight? Or is there a process in between that jump? Can you imagine making a million dollars in one year? How about losing a big portion of what you gained due to unknowns and blindspots? Would you have the courage and the fortitude to make it back?

Well, I can tell you that the journey to success and making a million dollars is a powerful one. My bank account jumped from around ten thousand dollars to over a half million in three months in the Spring of 2020. Then my stock account jumped from $150,000 to $800,000 in seven months in 2020/2021. I proceeded to give back a large portion of those gains due to blindspots in my new endeavor as a stock trader. I can tell you that the happiest I have ever been in this whole journey has been making sales in my suit business and base hits in my trading. In February of 2021, my stock account jumped about $140,000 in one day. Can you imagine going from having $10,000 to your name to one year later being a composite millionaire and making that much money in one day? It was surreal, and yes I was jumping around like crazy, literally.

It's experiences like that that changed my perspective of making and attracting wealth. I have felt the fear and danger of owing huge bills, the day-to-day struggle of making rent while living in a big city and going through the growing pains of a young entrepreneur, and I have also felt the thrill of making modest win-falls like these I am speaking of here.

As I look back on this journey that started in my 47,000-mile trek around the states in 2019 in my GLK 350, sleeping in my car and everywhere else, I can attribute the success that I have experienced to one major constant that transformed everything. My suits.

The way I feel when I get dressed every day is the most powerful constant that I have managed to build into my life. They say that powerful habits are the key to success, but I've never been one to make it a point to go to the gym or get up at a certain time. One thing I have done though is created myself and my powerful wardrobe very intentionally since 2017. It's been a serious journey. But along the way, even when my suits were expensive to pay for, I did it anyway. And building the garments that I have built, wearing them every day as I continue to take my journey, embracing each and every step, challenge, and opportunity in the process has made all the difference.

By becoming magnetic, I managed to magnetize my vision into fruition.

I never knew how I was going to make it here, I just knew and believed. I read a list of personal autosuggestions first thing every morning and last thing before shutting my eyes every night since March 1st of 2018 and I continue this process today. I confess that occasionally I miss a morning or a night if I'm entertaining, but not both, and I always continue to modify and add to this list. I know the power of the subconscious mind and I have found this to be the most direct way of accessing and influencing it so as to continue improving my life, character, and impact.

There is an old philosophical movie that I can recall watching several times. The film seems to delineate some of the most poignant truths and questions in life's great quest for meaning. That movie is called Waking Life. In the film, there is a quote that says we must be in a "constant state of departure while always arriving."

To me, this boils down to being present, being humble, and being real. Basing your life and your goals, in things that, in the words of my friend Jerry Lobozzo in his book Speak For Yourself, "contribute to the World Fix," makes all the difference. To do things for personal gain alone can never create fulfillment. However, attaching a bigger purpose behind everything you do while keeping your eyes on the bigger purpose, well that right there, that is key.

As they say before takeoff in almost every airplane, "first put on your oxygen mask before assisting someone next to you." The question that most people never ask or think about, is what do you do once you've already done that? What do you do once you've figured out how to make a million dollars? Is the real answer to go and figure out how to make ten, twenty, one hundred, or one billion dollars? Maybe.

All I know is that the greatest joy I've ever known is sharing something I have learned with someone else and watching them succeed as a result. It is for that reason that I am here to pay it forward and pass along a little known knowledge... An almost secret world, that, if you blinked, you could miss.

The Revolution Begins

Part 1 - Blonde

CHAPTER 1

ESCAPE THE DEPARTMENT STORE AND DRESS LIKE A KING FOREVER

"It isn't enough to think outside the box. Thinking is passive. Get used to acting outside the box."

- Tim Ferriss

Are you tired of traipsing around stores, malls, and shops trying to find your next set of duds? Is your wife annoying you to go to the store and dress better? How about online shopping? Are you tired of buying things online only to find out that it's nothing like you thought it would be?
Welcome to the club.

The majority of people do not enjoy the headaches of running around stores wasting precious downtime only to find themselves doing circles trying to find something over-the-top awesome.

As a clothier, I of course make all of my own shirts, suits, shorts, coats, you name it! The only garments I don't make for myself are my Calvin Klein boxers, my black jockey slim-fit stretch crew necks, and Happy Socks. Literally, the rest of my closet is composed of custom garments from my personal brand, Big Murphy's.

If I were to personally imagine the predicament of someone looking for a certain color shirt, jacket, or pants. Or a certain cut, style, heck, even someone looking to get ready for a wedding!

From my perspective, it would be akin to someone in Antarctica searching for a boat to California to buy avocados, meanwhile, I'm sitting on a beach in Mexico with avocado trees at home in my backyard.

Don't get me wrong, I've been that guy in Antarctica searching for the boat to California to buy avocados... And eventually, I found the supermarket, as most people usually do, but few have the fortitude to find the avocado trees.

Now to take this analogy one step further.. To say that you perhaps find a grocery store where you can buy these avocados... for say 3 maybe 5 dollars each (depending on inflation and demand). What if you knew how to get them from the comfort of your own home for less than 99 cents? Do you think you'd be making more guacamole? Heck, maybe you'd even sell guacamole! What if it could turn into a business that could in turn give you the freedom you've longed for all along!

I'm not sure about you, but I've heard avocados are healthy, and when it comes to what's healthy and good for you, it's always great to have more than enough to go around!

Now, I'm sort of beating around the bush, but you get the point.

CHAPTER 2

WHY WINDOW SHOPPING CAN CHANGE YOUR LIFE

"Synchronicity is an ever present reality for those who have eyes to see"

- *Carl Jung*

In 2016, I was visiting some friends in Prague, Czech Republic. I woke up from a dream and had an idea to make leather bags. I was led to a factory that made them as the person I was staying with had a neighbor who was a shoe cobbler who opened a factory making bags. About one year later the Big Murphy's brand was born and they made the bags. I launched the brand on the 67th floor of the Sears Tower in Chicago.

Building the concept around the brand took nearly 9 months

to perfect, like a baby getting ready to be born. The name came from an article I had found in my family's archives from my late grandmother Mimi's box of family history. It was a newspaper clipping from the 1930s about my great grandfather Charles W. Murphy or "Big Murphy" as he was called; a defense attorney for the bootleggers in the 1920s and 1930s in downtown Rochester.
Launching the brand in the Sears Tower was something that I did on an absolute shoestring budget. I can say without a doubt that its being brought to fruition on the day which it was, is something that must have been written in the stars many moons before my time.

It turned out that the day the Metropolitan club in the Sears Tower had given me to use the club's most preeminent suite to launch the brand was the same day that my great grandfather died in 1938. It also happened to be the same exact day that JFK was assassinated in 1963.
November 22nd... That was the day...

That was the date written on Big Murphy's death record that I found in the record archives in the downtown public library in Rochester, New York. It was the same day that 150 people from around the Chicago area came together to support me in launching my first truly successful endeavor.

The one that led me to become a full-time entrepreneur. First launched as a bag company, then to become a suit company, then to become a bag and shoe company again as well, and then to birth a mask company during the pandemic. All of this stemmed from a dream I had in Prague... one that I literally woke up from thinking that I'm going to find a way to make leather bags.

But before I had that dream I was busting my ass as a waiter, saving money to take that vacation to Prague, and hand sewing leather journals in my first business as an Artisan Entrepreneur.

It was on cold, hot, quiet, and crazy nights that I would return home at two or three in the morning after finishing my evening shift at one of Chicago's most famous downtown deep-dish pizza restaurants.

On an occasional night I would pass by a new menswear store that had popped up near to Water Tower plaza in Downtown Chicago, a stone's throw away from the restaurant I was working at.

I would go there and stare into the windows.

During the daytime, I would find reasons to pass by there and make conversation with the person working while observing the exquisite garments around the shop. I knew that I couldn't afford to make more than one or two suits on a waiter's wage, but I had a hunch that if only I could figure out how to manufacture those garments, that perhaps I would stand a chance to wear those garments and even sell them!

That would really be something. I looked in the mirror. I saw my future self flash before my eyes. I used to talk to the mirror a lot during those times, and I confess that I still do. Only then I had long hair and a long beard. I had no idea that what I was most attached to would one day set me free and send me into one of the most powerful transitions and transformations that I could even imagine.

But we'll get to that...

CHAPTER 3

WHY MENSWEAR BRANDS ARE TAKING BIG CITIES BY STORM

"When the student is ready the teacher will appear"

- Laozi

Walking around the city of Chicago and networking into the heart of the different business chambers of commerce, I began to notice other custom menswear stores popping up. I believe I counted at least five popular stores with two or more locations. I began to take note of similarities and differences between the store fronts, suits, and fabrics.

By this time I had found a mentor in Portugal and learned a thing or two about getting started in the business, but let me tell you, I was a LONG way from having a clue about how to truly make a quality garment with any form of consistent accuracy or real phenomenal quality. That was going to take several factories, remakes, pissed off clients, and hard days. But that was what I signed up for, and what I was determined to get through so I could become one of the best.

It was around that time that a new client of mine had migrated over to me from a guy he was currently working with who was associated with a company that I won't name here in this text. This particular company is known for sniper sales techniques ingrained in their culture of relentless door to door suit selling.

I had the good fortune of meeting this gentleman. He had all sorts of strange ideas about how the "avocados" were made, produced, and sold. And I had a very vague understanding of how incredibly premeditated and cold SALES can be for people who are out to make a quota or else! I couldn't blame him, though. For him, it was a corporate career. For me, it was a brand and a passion. One that finally bought me the freedom to live on my own terms, and work one hundred percent for myself since July 3rd of 2017; coincidentally the same day that my late grandmother "Mimi" had passed three years prior. She always believed in me, and so I decided to take the leap on the day of her passing and go ahead and believe in me 100% as well. It was from that day on that the journey truly accelerated.

I burned the ships and somehow in her words, "made like a bird and flew".

But back to the point here.... One thing I couldn't quite grasp is how little this guy selling almost a million dollars per year in suits, door to door, knew or rather didn't know about the business he was in.

I began to poke around and realized only a handful of amazing factories were pumping out the majority of the garments being designed, made, produced, and sold in downtown Chicago, and in all of the big cities where those five stores or so also had locations.

Little by little the entire thing began to click, and my understanding of one of the coolest businesses I know started to become crystal clear.

But more on that as we go...

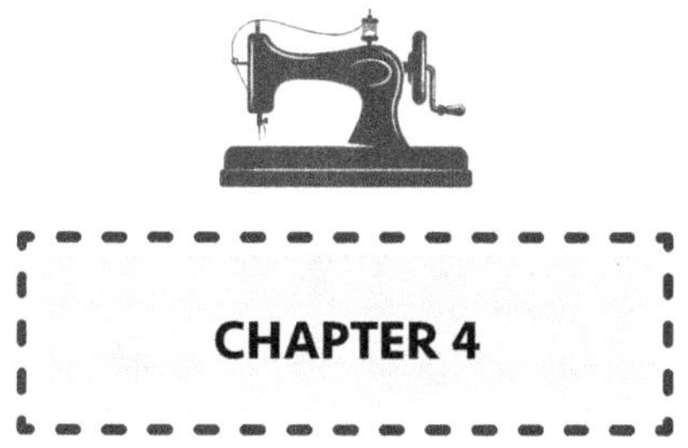

CHAPTER 4

WHY MA AND PA TAILORS WILL NEVER TRY TO SELL CUSTOM SUITS

"If the doors of perception were cleansed everything would appear as it is, infinite"

\- *William Blake*

In 2019, I was writing a three hundred and five-page suit manual about the suit business. But instead of being a broad text about the business and how I got into it, it was more of an actual textbook of how to be a "Next Level Clothier." It was titled Threads and later published on Amazon.

My Chicago tailor was a Ukrainian woman who had studied textile designs. She knew an absolute boatload about suits, dresses, fabric, and fit. She employed between six and twelve tailors at any given time and is known all around Chicago for her alterations business.

During a sit-down interview with her in 2019, I discovered her real connection to the greater Chicago custom suiting world. She had by chance bought her shop from a European tailor who had taught one of the most legendary Chicago custom suit makers to get into the business years before. She recalled in great detail what it was like to work with him and witness his success as a budding sensation and clothier in the 1980s, 1990s, and his more than one dozen store locations throughout the United States.

She confidently said to me, "Nathan, Big Murphys is going to be the most successful suit company in the entire United States of America."

She said that with such powerful conviction that I think I actually believed it.

We spent many, many mornings, afternoons, and evenings together in her shop, sorting out alterations, remakes, and requests for my growing suit clientele. Finally, after so many gut-wrenching mistakes and remakes, I was at my rope's absolute end and asked her, please, can we go through the measurements again one by one and please determine the absolute best way to avoid future remakes?

She agreed, and we spent hours making videos and perfecting what today has become the Big Murphy's measuring method.

After our interview, I turned and asked why she didn't want to sell custom suits? She showed me some correspondence with a factory I had heard of, and she simply told me that it was one of the most complicated and challenging processes that she had ever been through trying to design and produce suits with any success through that factory.

She preferred to continue with her alterations business instead of suffering the pain of throwing money in the wind only to watch it wash away with wrong garments and painful remakes.

She did sell shirts and suits in her store, but most of which were up to two or three hundred dollars, with the exception of her custom dresses sold even to celebrities for a hefty markup, but nonetheless made in her shop and not in a scalable factory.

She had found her niche and stuck with it. The truth is, she was a salt-of-the-earth person that was content with what was working for her. To learn to be a custom suit designer, build a large clientele, and produce in full-scale, in reality, was closer to being a high-performing financial planner than it was to being a tailor doing alterations.

Who knew!? And WTF? For real?

Yes... I know what you're thinking.

Part 2 - Box Pressed

THE BEST CLOTH MAY COME FROM EUROPE BUT THE BEST SUITS ARE NOT MADE IN ITALY

"Where there's smoke, there's bound to be mirrors"

- *Garry Trudeau*

I can still remember the first custom suit I ever tried on. It was late one night in Porto, Portugal. My friend owned a custom menswear store and asked me to try something on. When I felt the fabric, I could feel an almost electric current rush through my body, and suddenly my perspective shifted. Then when he told me the price, it shifted again. I had no idea what a jacket like that could cost. The amount was unfathomable to me at the time. And, to be honest, it would cost more than a good week's wages at the restaurant. But now we're going way back... This is back before I launched Big Murphy's and before the beginning of my transformation. Actually, this was one of the most important parts. A seed was planted.

Fast forward to the spring before launching Big Murphy's in 2016, and I found myself inside of that custom menswear store in downtown Chicago getting fit for my first truly custom blazer.

When the stylist told me the suits were made in China, I was appalled. "Really?" I said.

Yes...

She explained to me how the Chinese manufacturers were making a superior garment at this time. And that the customization options were fantastic. However, she also told me that remakes were very, very common and becoming a bit of a problem. I saw that she had a certain interesting platform in which she inputted my suit order. It looked straightforward but at the same time so complex.

I tried figuring out where they were made but had no luck. It was a sealed vault.

She told me the founders were software developers who had exited a previous venture and then started this new one.

I was very intrigued...

My journey continued, and at four in the morning, I found myself talking with a guy named Zdravko in Bulgaria via Skype. He was in an extremely loud factory where he was trying to explain their measuring process to me. It was literally the scariest and most exciting time of getting my suit business going, but let me tell you what, this part didn't end well.

Figuring out the measuring system was like cracking the code on a vault in a spy movie. The process was so bizarre that I was really worried about how my results would be, but instead, I continued on anyway. When I received some fabric swatches in the mail, they were clearly haphazardly thrown into an enormous cardboard box with try-on garments and a huge bag of buttons.

The swatches were damaged and desperately needed to be bound and organized. I spent one month bounding the fabrics with some creative wooden Dowling and some binder spines I bought online.

Then the buttons... forget about it. There were about three hundred of them. All in little baggies with hand-written serial numbers. I proceeded to sew each one onto cardboard cutouts that I used to make my own swatches. It took me three months to finally complete this task in my spare time before I even sold my first suit.

At the time, I couldn't even afford to make my own suits, so what did I do? I put on my Sunday best every day and pounded the pavement. From one networking evening to another. To 7am business breakfasts and brunches. I flew by the seat of my pants and sold thirty thousand dollars worth of suits before even making one Big Murphy's garment for myself.

It was funny, sometimes an order would go seamlessly well, and then at other times it would take a turn for the worst. Let me tell you what. If you don't keep your word with people and the deadlines of their suit's arrival, you can run into some serious problems.

I remember measuring a certain client in the outskirts of Chicago in the back room of his store. As I pulled out my measuring tape, he pulled out his gun. He gently placed it on the table. He didn't say much other than that it's a dangerous city, and his work involved a lot of dangerous people.

This didn't scare me. I could tell he was a great guy, as long as you stay on his good side of course.

About six weeks later, he was getting antsy for his suit. He needed it for a wedding, and he was demanding his money back. And when I say that he wanted it back, he got very angry and made some serious demands that I did not want to test. I had already paid the factory, and the suit was on its way, but was held up in customs. They needed to know the origin of absolutely every aspect of the suit. It was a mess.

I had very little to my name. Less than two thousand dollars in my account. But of course, I had to refund him his money. I sent him the thousand dollars back, and we were straight. The good news is that later when his suit finally came in, I went there to deliver it. I apologized and he wrote me a check for half of the original price as he had to go out and buy another suit. But at least we were on good terms.

This is just one story...

There were many scary stories like this in my journey. Many uncomfortable moments that caused me to learn the absolute quintessential nature of communication, expectation, and delivery.

I took notes and lessons in stride.

I realized that the quality of the suit and its deliverability are truly on the same level of importance.

My career as a clothier continued, and my reputation began to precede me. I became strongly recommended to people around the country, and when they asked where I was located, I simply said, "I come to you!"
And believe me, I did.

One more epic tale, and we'll get back to it here...

I left Rochester, New York, one afternoon and arrived at two o'clock in the morning at a client's house in Pekin, Illinois. I slept in his guest bedroom and then had coffee with him and his wife in the morning. He tried on his new suit and ordered another one.

At 10 AM the next morning, I was on the road to Tulsa, Oklahoma, where my assistant lived. He was receiving all shipments and prepping and sending out the suits so I could continue selling and living on the road.

I noticed that there seemed to be more wind than usual that day. And that driving from Rochester to Illinois, there was quite a bit as well. My Mom called me and told me to check the weather.

I pulled up the doppler and saw tornados all around me. I called my friend, and he said, you'll be fine... LOL. It wasn't fine...

Suddenly, the doppler showed a tornado rushing across the highway I was driving on. It had moved on the map and was now heading straight across the route I was on. I would refresh the screen, the tornado moving close with each refresh. And as I drove, I got closer. I looked around out of my car windows, and weirdly, the sky had turned black. It was the freakiest and scariest sky I had ever seen during the day. There was danger, and I knew it. I pulled off the highway immediately and into a Steak and Shake to ask what was going on. As soon as I got to the door, the woman pulled me inside and said, "Sir, you cannot go back outside. You have to stay in here." My entire livelihood was in my car. My samples, computer, everything. It was my last hope to make my life work as an entrepreneur.

Huddled in the Steak and Shake bathroom hallway with about twelve people, my life changed. I could feel danger like I had never felt before. An hour and a half went by, and they cleared us to sit down. So, I assessed the safety of leaving. Luckily my car wasn't damaged. But, as it turned out, it was an F4 tornado, and it passed by less than one mile from us and ripped everything to shreds in its path.

Something or someone saved my life that day. Probably my Mom, LOL. Without her calling, I might not have checked the weather. Anyway, I drove out of there at about 120 MPH and didn't stop until I got to Tulsa. My friend laughed and said, "Yeah, I forgot to tell you that it's tornado season." I was like, oh, "Thanks for that small detail." LOL. Focker.

I needed an oil change the following day and went to a local spot. Believe it or not, I made fast friends with the owner, a young and impressive entrepreneur, and the next morning I was measuring him for a suit in the back office of his auto shop. Again, he pulled a gun out of his pocket. I wasn't worried, but it was interesting to see. We even made some measuring adjustments for his holster.

That same day at noon, I drove from Tulsa, Oklahoma, through the night to Sarasota, Florida. I slept in my car at a rest stop in Alabama and continued after about four hours of off-and-on sleep. Why was I driving straight through? Well, I had a very important client to fit, and if I couldn't arrive by a certain date, they weren't going to be able to do it. It wasn't just anyone, though. I was on my way to make a custom suit for Ron Klein, inventor of the magnetic strip on the credit card and many other earth-shattering inventions that changed the world and all of our lives. He was a famous inventor. There was an entire program dedicated to him on the discovery channel.

I was determined to get him as my client!

I arrived in Tampa, showered at a marina where my family friends have a boat, and headed to the appointment. By the time I got back to sleep on the boat, I literally needed scotch tape to tape my eyelids open just to stay awake. Ok, I didn't tape my eyelids open, but I did drink more caffeine than was healthy and did everything else you can imagine a crazy person driving around for more than twenty-four hours straight, alone in a car would do. LOL.

As you can see, I earned my stripes.

Now... Back to it.

CHAPTER 6

WHY THE IBERIAN PENINSULA WILL ALWAYS BE THE BEST AT ONE THING

"Each contact with a human being is so rare. So precious, one should preserve it."

- *Anais Nin*

As my suit business began to flourish, I got myself an office. I didn't even have a lease on an apartment, but somehow I had an office. I had decided it was better to sleep on couches and in cars than it was to be tied to any one place with a lease. So I wasn't... Anyway, this is after I left Chicago in 2018 and moved to Portugal, only to find that my suit business needed some serious improving and increasing before I could live there full-time. So, I did the logical thing and flew by the seat of my pants.

Then in 2019, I met my tribe, a group of young professionals that happened to go to my same high school. I knew one of them vaguely from my high school years, but I had never met the others. I began making suits for them and frequenting their office. It was neat. They had a dog named Louie, or Luigi as we affectionately call him, and the entire building seemed to have an absolute zest for the best stuff on earth. Sex, drugs, and rock and roll? No, not really. More like chess, lunch, booze, and custom clothes. Real degenerates, I know. LOL.

Over the better half of a year, I got to know them pretty well, and one day I asked them about an office that was full of filing cabinets from floor to ceiling.
I can still remember my client/buddy's response, "Why, do you want it?"

I did... It all started to click.

So, I did the natural thing and bought a white couch, four wine barrels, and made a custom desk. I began decorating the office at night, and the guys would stop by and say, WTF? This is crazy. They started creating nicknames for me. Natedogg, or Nasty, which I don't particularly like but hey, it sort of stuck! They were all real ballbusters, as you can probably tell from their choice of titles for me. There was one guy who called me Nate the Great, though. That was a little better. But everyone seems to use the prior two, lol.

Anyway, during the assembly of this great convergence of awesomeness, I realized that my late great grandfather, Charles W. Murphy, who the Big Murphy's brand was named after, literally worked his entire life in the building next door. And here I was in a law building full of defense attorneys and other mavericks. Of course, when stars align, it's rather obvious, and this was one of those obvious and awesome moments.

As I got better and better and my business kept growing, I began to think back to my early days when I launched the Big Murphy's brand in the Sears Tower on that ominous night.

I can still remember searching for the perfect tagline. I had finished golfing at the Chicago nine-hole trek along the lake and remembered something about a book called the Devil in the White City. I was trying to find a way to connect a Rochester defense attorney who defended bootleggers in the 1920s and 1930s, including Al Capone's regime... true story... to the Windy City, CHITOWN, Chicago.

I was determined to make it a seamless connection.

I went home and downloaded that book on audible. At the time, I was still hand sewing leather notebooks and leather goods. I spent the entire night... about five hours listening to the book in my crazy apartment that was built like a boat and was even featured in an article in the Chicago Reader in 2013 in an article called Dreaming Big in Small Spaces. And that night, I was truly dreaming big.

The book talked about how Chicago had been planning to host the world's fair. There were architectural demands that were outside of what was then possible, from an engineering standpoint.

But as they say, "necessity is the mother of invention," and so one brave architect made a daring statement and when I looked up the historical significance of it, it became brandished in my brain. He said, "Make no small plans for they have no magic to stir one's blood." Wow, I said... That was it.
Big Murphy's, Make No Small Plans.

And so that's what I did. Making no small plans, I launched the Big Murphy's brand on the 66th and 67th floor of the Sears / Willis tower on November 22, 2016. One hundred years after Big Murphy himself graduated from Syracuse law. And the picture I used for the brand was a photo of his graduating class from 1916. So, logically, I made the bag collection that I was launching
and called it the 100 Year collection. Then I found out there was the Irish spring in Ireland in 1916, and my mind was blown... the number of coincidences happening was startling, to say the least.

So yeah, I was thinking back on all of that and recalling that while Big Murphy's launched as a custom bag brand, we barely sold any bags. Maybe 7 or 10 at most in the entire time. Of course, I had pivoted to suiting and realized that was a need, not a want, and that's where I found the success for the brand.

But was it true that we couldn't also succeed as a leather goods brand as well? Shoes and bags?

Well, that's when I looked back into my contacts in the Iberian Peninsula and realized I had connected with one of the most cutting edge factories making the most high-end and highest-quality shoes in all of the classic men's designs. So, I connected with them, and the rest is history. Over the the next two years, we rolled the whole thing out and now have more than one thousand shoe designs on our website and a three-dimensional design tool that allows you to make the most custom versions of your shoes imaginable.

But I didn't stop there... If you'll notice on the front of the Big Murphy's website that Big Murphy is holding a bag. That bag was photoshopped into his hand. But for some weird reason, his hand was positioned almost perfectly to receive the bag. It was like it was meant to be. We started as a bag company, and it was important to me that we continue as one.

I went back to the drawing board and, over the course of the following two years, I brought to fruition one of the most phenomenal briefcases in existence, and you guessed it, it's now available in 3D as well.

WOW, that was an endeavor, let me tell you... but the adventure is still only just beginning.
We'll get back to that in just a bit...

CHAPTER 7

WHY A NICE SET OF TITS AND A WORLD-CLASS CAR COLLECTION CAN SELL $10,000 SUITS

"Curvy hips, red lips, and a dangerous pair of eyes"
- *JM WONDERLAND*

Now, I'm sure you've seen some pretty powerful Instagram influencers touting some serious style, but some are doing it at another level. I'm talking about custom menswear, Rolls Royces, Porches, classy-vintage sports cars, yachts, and island hopping around Europe. I mean, there's one guy, in particular, that does all this, and he's even a family man to boot!

On the other hand, there are secret snipers like a chick I once met in the heart of Manhattan's financial district in the lobby of a hedge fund. I saw her walking in with some suits she was obviously delivering to a client. She was very attractive and very assertive. Two can play at that game, I thought to myself, but I was missing one thing. My swag was not her swag. And honestly, I'm not a competitive person. To be honest, of course, I didn't want her poaching my client, but there was and always is more than enough to go around. You see, this industry has many forms and comes in many packages. I've met female clothiers with breasts the size of my head and client lists that resemble huge phonebooks, and I've met down-to-earth immigrants with the work ethic of an absolute horse. But none of that has ever intimidated me. I can always see their product. And based on my journey of hard knocks getting into this business and the more than half a dozen factories I have personally worked with, I can tell immediately what's going on behind the curtain and under the hood.

But every suit is not the same, and everyone's taste is indeed a bit different. It's also what we're told and shown to be "cool" that becomes the benchmark.

Take, for instance, that first guy with the insane toys and compound to boot. He brings his clients through a crazy experience. He imitates the making of a "bespoke suit," attaching the jacket sleeves at the end, and ends up making all of his clients wear a roped shoulder that, to me, just looks forced and pukey. But there's an ass for every seat, as my grandfather would say. And boy, oh boy, do his clients pay. This guy charges whatever he wants. Jackets for $10K; suits for $20K. There is no limit on luxury there. And his clientele happily obliges with the prices.

But what is the real difference between a top-notch, bespoke, custom suit from Big Murphy's for $2500-$3500 and his for $10,000? One word. Perception. And our suits, sorry to say, are superior. Why? They're built with the client in mind. No standard roped shoulder over here. Just the best fit and image for your personal brand, not ours.

Now, back to the tits.

While I know this sounds ridiculous, there is a fine line between paying for an escort and buying a high-end custom suit. At least if you live in Manhattan.
Let me tell you what.
I've known very attractive female clothiers capable of commanding prices that would rival even those of our friend with the insane compound and car collection. Heck, he has yachts, pro soccer players, and he lives the life of a full-blown superhero. He's even a dad. I think it's awesome!

But back to the tits - LOL.

Some men just desperately want to be told what to wear, how to dress, made to feel important, and they don't mind swiping their Amex black to do it. It's like buying a Dom Pérignon for $50K. You're not focused on the price. If you're buying at that level, it's because price no longer enters the equation.

Interestingly, those suits they are peddling are no better than our friend's suits with the car collection and compound. It's all about perception.

What is better, though?

You guessed it. OR, actually, you probably have no idea because both of those are pretty awesome. But yeah. What's better is: Accountability. Reliability. Fairness.

It's one thing to get a customer. It's another to keep a client.

PRO ATHLETES PAY BUT DO YOU REALLY NEED THEM TO CREATE A TOP SUIT BUSINESS?

"If opportunity doesn't knock, build a door"
- *Milton Berle*

Now, after that exec spending $10K or $15K on each suit finally comes to his senses or has some sort of moment of spiritual sobriety, I don't know – maybe his wife calls him, and he realizes that while he hasn't physically crossed the line with his clothier, he might have been emotionally cheating, just a little. It's around that time that I swoop in. Honest, upfront, and straightforward.

I always feel bad when I hear the stories of custom clothiers taking guys completely to the cleaners. How they walked into one of those downtown suit shops only to get wham-bam-thank-you-mammed. They come to me all jammed up and still emotionally hungover from how they either overspent or overspent and still got a crappy product. Believe it or not, the industry standard is not to deliver great clothes. It's to make quotas and see people in units and packages. It's all about a bottom line. And to be honest, that's just not for me. When I begin working with a client, sometimes, we spend the entire afternoon just getting to know one another.

Here, real quick. A long time ago, I was in Maryland. There was a guy in Long Island that wanted a suit. I remember driving three and a half to four hours to see him. Only to spend four hours getting to know one another, then having dinner, and finally doing measurements and designing his first garments. I then got back in the car and drove from ten at night until two in the morning to get back to Maryland; a place I was based in for a brief time (couch surfing / brand building days).

I mean, if a guy is busy and just wants to get down to it and doesn't have much time, I can do that too. Heck, I most recently measured that guy I told you about in a hotel bar at two in the morning while a chick he was sort of picking up waited. It took me about 25 minutes, and by the end, he paid me via cc, and off he went. He trusted me with the design, and six weeks later, he received a beautiful shirt and suit, and he even told me that the chick he was picking up was now his steady girlfriend. WOW, I thought to myself...

In the back of my head, I was thinking, man, I bet that woman saw an advancing man. A man that, while he was a bit overweight and balding... he was a keeper, a hard worker, and a go-getter.

And there was one of those moments of pure gold. When I realized that I was doing what I'm fashioned to do. Anyway... enough of the sappy stuff, back to it.

Part 3 - Maduro

CHAPTER 9

WHY YOUR LOCAL SUIT COMPANY IS RIPPING EVERYONE OFF, AND HOW YOU STAND TO PROFIT

"Honesty is the fastest way from preventing a mistake from turning into a failure"
- *James Altucher*

Ever walked into a car dealership with a big stupid smile on your face and walked out the same day with your brand new car only to wake up a week later to realize you got a 16 percent interest rate and a car payment you can barely afford? I hope you have not, but I personally have. And let me tell you what, it simply sucks.

It's just sales, right? They're just doing their job, aren't they? No. No. No. No.

Moral hazard is a real thing.
And when you sell someone a monthly bill they can't afford that expires in five or seven years, you are definitely entering the territory of moral hazard.

I have unfortunately had to field the complaints of many disgruntled chaps walking around with their tails between their legs after being stung by a local clothing regime. They're the best because they've been around the longest, right? Wrong.

All big companies that grow old do not always grow up. And when you put your interest before your customers, you're going to learn a hard lesson. And that may just be that they don't want to work with you anymore. They might feel like they're being slid into a series of smiles and smoke and mirrors until they reach the checkout and find a bill for $10K instead of $2K.

But hey, that's life! You pay for what you get, you might say. Ok. Ok. But pigs get fed, and hogs get slaughtered.

Is it really all bad? Charging a premium for a great product? Of course not!

Look at Lamborghini. Did you know that in 2017 I had the pleasure of sitting next to Tonino Lamborghini, the son of the founder of Lamborghini motors? Yes, that's right, the world-famous car company. The Lambos. The trophy touted by so many Instagram influencers once they have "made it."

I can remember something that Tonino Lamborghini told the entire audience that day at the event. He said the secret behind the success of his brand, or any brand with serious curb appeal like Lamborghini has, is to get people to save up a boatload of money just to happily hand it over for what you give them in return. That is the secret recipe of the secret sauce.

Again, what's the difference between this local company I may be referring to here and Big Murphy's? Well, I believe we make a superior product as many of their molds are outdated, but that's just a personal opinion.

I do, of course, see my competition's clothing when their clients come to me with sob stories about what they overpaid for and, in some cases, were underdelivered. The garments are often too structured with bulky shoulders and boring standard lining cuts. They don't even bother to give a French cut!

Not to be confused with French Cuff. A French cut is when the inside jacket pocket is also made from the fabric of the suit, causing the whole suit to lay better and prevent the pockets from sagging. Over time, without a French cut, the garments are severely compromised. Now, on a manufacturing level, do you know the cost difference between a French cut and a standard lining cut?

Ten bucks.

Yup, that's it. Pound for pound, that's just penny wise and pound foolish.

At Big Murphy's, I decided from the outset, no matter what, we don't cut corners. We do not look at the bottom line. We do not compromise on quality, and all of our lapel buttonholes are hand-sewn. That is a Big Murphy's trademark.

It's amazing how sticking to a few simple principles and offering your services at a fair price eventually wins you a fair share of the market. Now, I'm not saying you're not owed a profit. Of course, profit is healthy. But moral hazard is not.

At the end of the day, there is a market for Lambos, and there is a market for Teslas. And in this case, Big Murphy's is a Tesla, and electric cars are the future. So, here I am, paying it forward.

And pretty soon, if you don't blink, you might even find out what's really under the hood in the clothing business.
But more on that later. We've still got more ground to cover.

CHAPTER 10

WHY THE NEW YORK KNICKS CLOTHIER GOT FIRED AND WHY YOU COULD REPLACE HIM

"Victory comes from finding opportunity in problems"
- *Sun Tzu*

When you think about the person making custom suits for heavy hitters like professional athletes, you might think that they'd be heavily vetted and almost need a background check to get anywhere near them, right? Think again. Back in 2019, I got a phone call from a current client down in the Long Island area. He had wanted to put me in touch with his best friend from high school, who was strongly affiliated with the New York Knicks. To respect privacy, he asked me to keep his position with the organization a secret. Anyway, he's a very strong man with a powerful stature. And I soon came to find out in person just how stacked this gentleman was.

I can recall driving to Long Island from Rochester, New York. I left early in the morning, around 6 AM, to make the 3 PM appointment. When I arrived at his home, he told me he had a clothier that used to make his shirts and suits. He made reference to his complacency and sudden loose communication style. It surprised my soon-to-be loyal client that someone he had passed so much business to could have so quickly forgotten where he had come from. You see, this new phenomenal client of mine remembered the very first time he had interacted with this young suit salesman. He explained to me his exuberant style and character. He also explained his ability to sell. Nowhere in the conversation did I hear about his credentials. I then asked what company the gentleman had worked for to confirm my hunch, and in fact, my intuition was correct. Of course, I cannot name this door-to-door suit company's name as not to defame them nor cause any disrespect, but the word on the street is that they are better in sales than in clothing. Sure, they can make a suit fit (some of the time – LOL), but can they take the time to treat you like anything more than just a number in their quota, let alone care about your pocketbook?

After hearing this gentleman's disgruntled complaints about having felt disrespected and under-appreciated, I took the time to show him my book, CLOTHES MORE DEALS, The Art Of Framing Possibility. I, of course, gave him a copy. I then took out my 305-page manual, THREADS, Next Level Clothiers. Through the manual, I explained to him the Big

Murphy's process for framing opportunity through personal branding and the frame control that powerful personal garment details can give us. We probably talked for a good forty-five minutes to an hour before I even got into the crux of our suits, fabrics, styles, and pricing. When our meeting had concluded, he made it clear that I would have to prove myself on this first order, but once I did that, I would have a loyal customer moving forward with no frets and no quirks. And to this day, he has been that exactly; a straightforward, clear, sharp, and concise person to do business with. Of course, when he told me that story, I took some notes. Unfortunately, it's human nature to get sloppy, greedy, and complacent. It's a shame that once handed such a phenomenal opportunity on such a golden platter, someone would screw it up like that.

"One more thing," he said as I was leaving. "Wear that suit on every first client meeting. That thing is really strong and sends a message that you mean business and know what you're doing."

Now, what did it take to get a golden opportunity like this? To be at the right place, at the right time? Well, sure I was, in some regards. But really, I was just showing up, dressing up, and continuing to build in a high vibration day in and day out, doing my best to do what I said I was going to do. That's it. Did I ever make a mistake along the way? You bet I did! A lot of them! But I find that people tend to be forgiving when you show them that you really care and that whatever happened wasn't your intention at all and that, on the contrary, you're going to make it up to them. And it's usually at those times that I send someone a little something extra. It all depends on the occasion. Most of the time, it's a shirt or a tie. Either way, I own up to it and make it right. Period.

They say that there exists a strength between loose ties. And when you think about it, the majority of clients I have been recommended to were people who I had never met before the day that I first fitted them. However, the great lengths that I ventured to go see them, spend time with them, treat them like a human being, and then make and deliver them amazing clothes – well, that has made all the difference.

So, do I make clothes for the New York Knicks? Yes, I do. Do I make them for the players? I can not speak to that, and even if I did, it's irrelevant to the bigger point being made here. I make great clothes for great people, period. And referrals are always welcome and key. Wink Wink.

Foreshadow...

WHY EVERY GUY KNOWS A GUY AND HOW TO BECOME THAT GUY

"The currency of real networking is not greed but generosity"

- *Keith Ferrazzi*

Once my crazy wine barrel desk was built in the downtown of Rochester, New York, I began to get a lot of traffic. With a lot of law firms nearby, people began to drop in. One thing led to another, and before you know it, there was a new guy in town. New guy? No, not a different guy, it was me – I was the new guy. And, wow, I was grateful to have landed again and to be once more putting down roots and building a community. Back in Chicago, my community was pretty tight-knit. Between my morning breakfast BNI groups, downtown chamber of commerce, and the Metropolitan Club in the Sears Tower, I had really created a vast network. But in a city that big, it's tough to really find the kind of pals that'll treat you like a brother – so, wow was it awesome finding that. I think that every human being longs to find a community. A group of like minds to mastermind with but also to keep each other in check and on point. That's what the real value of a solid community is. There's an African proverb that says, "if you want to go fast, go alone, if you want to go far, walk with others."

I can also hear the words of one of my top mentors echoing in my head, Dr. Greg Reid. He says, "You are a reflection of the five people you spend the most time with," and so, essentially, you better pick them carefully. Without realizing it, I had somehow transformed my hometown into a vacuum for success. Each and every day that they arrived earlier to the office, I realized that maybe I should get up a bit earlier. And maybe I should try this or that. And little by little, my business grew, and along with my goofy nickname, that grew my business as well. It really became like a family, and by that time, I realized that my business wasn't the only thing doing better. I personally was doing better. The truth is, the journey of driving around selling suits and flying by the seat of my pants was taking its toll. It definitely was the path less traveled, but in the end, I knew that that was the one I'd decided to take in life a long time ago...

Heck, I decided to become an exchange student and live in the Czech Republic for a year when I was 18 years old after high school and before college. Somewhere along the way, I think I just got used to taking a different route – lol.

Speaking of routes... I can recall a phone interview with one of the most successful clothiers I'd ever met. He was a guy in his mid-forties living in New Jersey. I knew that he was a hard worker, but I had no idea how he'd grown his suit empire. Somehow, he had single-handedly figured out how to sell over a million dollars a year in suits with no business card, website, or employees. He said he did it all while playing golf and poker. I didn't understand. He said, "Yeah, I basically play golf all the time, and most of my suit appointments are twenty to twenty-five minutes long." I couldn't believe it. He was a straightforward guy, and I could see why people liked him. There was no beating around the bush. He found a strategy and stuck with it for over twenty years, and believe it or not, it made him a millionaire pretty quick. And yup, you guessed it. He's the epitome of the guy that everyone knows. The cool thing is that I also now have a solid group of clients in New Jersey, and people are calling me their guy, and I drop in and out a few times a year to play golf, smoke cigars, and have dinner.

I guess I'm taking a page out of his book.

I mean if you're not learning from those around you, then what are you waiting for?

CHAPTER 12

GETTING PAID AND GETTING LAID HAVE TWO THINGS IN COMMON

"Life is too short to wear boring clothes"

- Unknown

They say that every woman likes a sharply dressed man, and let me tell you, they do! But I'm not talking about women in the plural sense, or at least not now anyway, lol. In my case, I met the girl of my dreams at a wine bar in Portugal. Being the guy that I am, I was, of course, wearing a Big Murphy's custom three-piece suit and a black overcoat with a velvet Chesterfield collar and black suede elbow pads. The suit was also black and made with what I like to call Big Murphy's blue thread. It was my go-to suit at the time. And she confessed later that what I was wearing was an instant clincher. The next day when I went to have coffee with her, I picked her up wearing another one of my go-to three pieces. She said that it was then and there that she knew how the day would end. To me, she was the most beautiful girl I had ever seen. I can remember shaking at times; her beauty was so powerful. But at the end of the day, she said yes! No, we didn't get married. Not yet anyway. But she did say yes to coming upstairs, and at the moment, that was a huge win! ;)

I guess what I'm getting at here is the power of first impressions. You're either setting yourself up for success or failure in any situation you encounter, and the choice is always yours. You can either choose to do things that swing the odds of success in your favor, or you can choose to believe that the little things don't matter. Well, let me tell you what. That could not be further from the truth. It's the little things that make all the difference. As Al Pacino in Any Given Sunday says, "Life is this game of inches." He says that "The inches that we need are all around us. They're in every break of the game, every minute, and every second... And when you add up all those inches, that's gonna be the f**kin difference between winning and losing. Between living and dying." And that, my friends, is the truth.

As you know from an earlier chapter in this book, I am also a stock trader. Let me tell you what. In that game, every millisecond counts. Every single thing you do to plan your day out for success in the market is key. From the times you take your trades, to the phone calls you field, to the times when you take bathroom breaks. It all matters, and optimizing yourself for success is the key to making your airplane fly.

Speaking of which, each and every clothier has his or her own process of designing and making clothing. I liken it to flying an airplane. Now, if you're trying to fly a regular flight, you can probably do so on autopilot. But if you're looking to push the limits and be the best you can be, you're going to need to know your aircraft intimately well. You're going to need to know how every little aspect works to make this thing really perform. That's part of the art of making great clothes. Building custom suits is hard. It's not easy. It takes fortitude, humility, patience, and wisdom. But once you master it, it's the coolest skill I know that also makes great money!

Imagine getting paid just to wear cool and empowering clothes all the time. Getting paid to make yourself new clothing and naturally attract clients everywhere you go! You could even do this in addition to what you already do!

That's my experience of life as a clothier, and it only keeps getting better.

Like that one time at band camp... lol. No, let's skip that scene, haha.

Part 4 -Churchill

CHAPTER 13

WHY IT'S OKAY TO NEVER GROW UP AND GET A REAL JOB

"Tenacity is the ability to hang on when letting go appears the most attractive"

- *Unknown*

In 2012, I graduated from Loyola University of Chicago. I had an absolutely phenomenal academic experience and loved my teachers and subjects. But at the end of the day, I had no real idea of how to make money coming out of college. I studied philosophy, journalism, and Spanish literature, and somehow managed to do a major in all of them in four years, including one year of study abroad in Argentina. I've never been an overachiever by any means, but I have been a very curious person with a large intellectual appetite. That doesn't make me smart, but curious and committed, yes.

Anyway, during my year abroad in Buenos Aires, Argentina, in 2010-2011, I had a mega lightbulb that went off in my head. I thought that perhaps there could be a way to inspire the sort of transformation that I had had through student exchange and study abroad in others. I thought that just maybe I could do something to pay it forward and also get paid to do it. My notion of doing business was pretty elementary at the time, but hey, we all start somewhere!

So, there I am in Buenos Aires, standing on the rooftop of my house, staining pages of blank white paper with a bucket of coffee and then letting them dry on my rooftop. See, I had an idea to make leather notebooks and sell that at the art fair in San Telmo. Around then, I had been very interested in this backpack that I was sewing and carrying around during my college years. At the time, I was somewhat of a cross between Jack Kerouac and Johnny Depp. I would walk into stores, and people would say, you know who you remind me of? That Johnny Depp guy from Pirates of the Caribbean. LOL.

Yup, that was me. Long hair, long beard, with a lot of curiosity and drive.
I remember sitting on that rooftop outside of my room and dreaming of building a powerful brand through a notion of 'Getting Lost To Find Yourself,' and so I called it, WalknTalk. That brand taught me a lot.

First of all, I sold my fender Strat in the basement of a bar in

Buenos Aires, bought $700 worth of leather, and shipped it up to the states. My idea was that I was going to make these leather notebooks and sell them. I was in my senior year at Loyola, making notebooks, and thinking non-stop about how I would sell them and make this work after college. I'm not sure what I was thinking, really, but I dove straight in, no job, no nothing. With a couple thousand bucks and a tiny mercy loan from my father, I got started. I even built a mobile notebook stand out of a 1970's Schwinn bike. I got a permit from the city of Chicago that said, "Not Food Not Junk." Talk about a special category to be in, LOL. My gosh... I look back and think. What was I thinking?!
But you know what, this is my story, and that was my journey.

I managed to get into a few newspapers, magazines, and online articles. I sold at art fairs around Chicago and New York. I guess you can say I was a Maker. And boy did I make. After

working with the Amish in Ohio, I started hand sewing the leather notebooks myself one at a time in my apartment in Chicago. In total, I made about 5000 of them by hand.

But one day, while I was sewing at my bench, looking out over Lake Michigan, I was listening to an audiobook (of course... as always), and what it had to say clicked. It was Tim Ferriss's Four Hour Work Week. "Escape the 9-5 and Join the New Rich." I found it interesting that he had been an exchange student as well. However, the concepts in the book that spoke to me most were not how to become rich, but rather about how to outsource and simplify my business. So, with those wheels in motion, I went to work. I realized that only one or two of my products actually made sense to outsource and make in quantity. And so I tried. And I tried. And the notebooks were awesome, and they still are! But there is a difference between wants and needs, and what I thought was cool and what people actually wanted.

You see, every entrepreneur has to learn the lesson of getting past their own ego. Letting go of what they think will sell, and instead ask other people. Go test it out.

So, with that idea, I did. And after a while, I came to the conclusion that what I was doing was a hobby, not a business.

It was then that, through a series of connected events in Portugal a few years later, I got acquainted with custom men's suits and clothing. The good thing was that I had already learned how to run a little business. I knew how to market and sell things online, and I even had assembled a whole digital team to help bring my vision to fruition. What I needed now was a product that people actually wanted.

And then, like magic, little by little, I began to understand the custom menswear business. I began to meet people and attract the way forward. And real quick, I always had style, just more of a free-thinking academic philosopher vibe.

The more I held onto the past and my old way of doing business, the harder I had to work. Don't get me wrong, I LOVED making notebooks, and it was fun. But it took a lot of time and energy. And I needed to transition into a business that I could do anywhere, anytime, with anyone and somehow be great and get paid to do it!

It was in 2016 that these wheels really began to turn in motion. In 2017, I was like a toddler crawling. In 2018, I was taking my first steps. And then, in the Fall of that year, I made the brave move to do a 180 and literally leave it all behind. My ten-year stint in Chicago was over. I realized that my life there was inefficient and expensive. Like a stock without buyers, or a plane overloaded with cargo, I saw the problem, and I was ready to fix it.

So, I did the natural thing and put everything I owned in my Aunt's basement, simplified my life into two suitcases, and flew to Portugal to turn thirty and start my next decade living in the place I'd always wanted to live. Wow, was it ever freeing. I had built a small and mighty customer base, but my suit business still needed fine-tuning. It was then, in the Spring of 2019, that I came back and drove those 47,000 miles around the country selling suits and building my business. Don't ask me how, but it worked.

And from then on, simplifying overhead and unnecessary excessive styles of living/costs has been my guide for flying that plane. You see, in the beginning, to get the plane off the ground and be able to support myself I needed to lighten my aircraft. But once I got airborne, the entire picture came clearly into view.

Now looking back, I probably could have skipped the challenging parts of waiting tables until two AM while building my businesses, but the skills I acquired in that restaurant were priceless. Believe it or not, I once had a section of five tables, and I spoke to them all in different languages. Czech, Spanish, Portuguese, Slovak, and English. It was wild. But most of all, I did it my way.

Now, I'm telling you all of this so that you can see it wasn't easy. I struggled like crazy for the better half of a decade. But I made it through, and now what? Now my life is my own. My clients are scattered around the world, primarily in the US, and I get paid to do what I love to do.

And thanks to COVID, we even do virtual fittings now!

What a dream. I always knew it was possible, but now I'm living it. Who would have thought that a clothier driving around the states like a madman could live a semi-retired lifestyle in one of the coolest ex-pat countries in the world, all while living in his dream apartment and getting paid to do what he was already going to do? ... Design great clothes.

And you can too! But we'll get to that...

HOW TO BE A LION IN A WORLD OF LAMBS

"Leaders with no discernment can do tremendous damage in a short amount of time"

- Mel Lawrence

For a long time, I spent much of my time asking others for their opinion, and I still do! It's great to get feedback. But, more important than feedback is the ability to discern things for yourself. To learn to make decisions and stick by them. In my recent endeavor of becoming a stock trader, I learned that this behavior had to stop. Asking other traders what they thought about a certain stock or when to get out of a stock etc., was all not only a bad idea, it was very dangerous. I got that lesson to the tune of several hundred thousand dollars. Now, looking back on my humble beginnings, you might say, lucky guy, at least you had the hundreds of thousands in the first place! Not so fast. It's all relative.

Now, it wasn't until I became consistent in my conviction of when to buy and when to sell a stock in my trading that I began to really find consistent results. And the funny thing is making money in trading is all about mastering your emotions and sticking to your decisions.

In business, it's similar but different. If you're considering making a bold move, like moving out of the country with no "concrete" job contract, etc., or quitting your job to open a business, then be prepared to avoid the long list of crabs that will most certainly be "concerned and worried" about you and whether or not it's going to work out. They're going to be "scared" for you. The funny thing is that the process one must endure to transform their life, whether personally, professionally, or whatever, is always one that will require a leap of faith. But if you jump with full faith, the universe will catch you. But you have to really jump, not sort of jump.

You have to burn the ships. Like when sailors went out to fight and take land. They would burn the boats so that there was no option of returning. That's the only way to the other side. And yes, it's going to be messy, hard, challenging, and at times, completely fucked up. Like when my bank accounts were all overdrawn in 2017, and I was driving a Mercedes with a 16% interest rate and realized my girlfriend had taken my iPhone charger with her to the airport. So, I needed to count $9 out of my change jar to buy a new charger from 7 ELEVEN where they had just jacked the price. I mean, that is what I call a fucked up situation.

Granted. They were my choices that led me there. I wouldn't wish that on anyone, but I'll tell you what. There is nothing like a situation like that one to teach you some very valuable lessons. And if I had to do it all over again, I wouldn't change a thing. I always knew that one day I would be laughing at this and that I'd get past it.

The key is perseverance.

I like this one quote in the film Robin Hood. It appears on the handle of an Excalibur sword. It says, "Rise and rise again, until lambs become lions."

I rest my case.

You'll make it.

If you're looking for a way out. I can help you.

Stuck in a job you hate? A boring lifestyle you'd like to change? Trust me, custom clothes are powerful. They changed my life, and they can change yours.

More on that soon.

CHAPTER 15

INSTAGRAM IS FOR TIME SUCKERS BUT WE STILL WATCH THE REELS

"We cannot despair of humanity, since we ourselves are human beings"

- *Albert Einstein*

Have you ever noticed how much time we stare at our screens on a day-to-day basis? I mean, it's pretty ridiculous. And me as a stock trader, forget about it. It's rough. But I manage it and take breaks.

Now I'm not a computer programmer, but I know we're being programmed every single day. Especially by social media. We're not just being programmed, but we're being conditioned. What to think, what to wear, who's hot, who's not? What to give a f**k about. What to not give a F**k about. Etc.

But what if we could beat the algorithm and bend it to our will? I'm as guilty of Instagram-binging as anyone, but at least follow some motivation accounts. Or heck, follow some other ones too! Don't be afraid to follow people you don't know. I'm annoyed that there's even a stigma around that. It's funny; I bump into and find so much stuff on Instagram. I learn things all the time. But I only do so because I use my higher awareness to follow the signs and synchronicities as they present themselves. And I'm not talking about stupid ads that are retargeted toward me. I'm talking about following hunches and climbing down the rabbit hole.

The question is, where does it lead, and how far does it go?

"Life is an adventure, or it's nothing" - Helen Keller

We are here to live. And to me, living is learning. And learning is living as well! I believe I've already mentioned audiobooks here quite a bit. I don't just listen to books on Audible. I study them. I use that as my personal library, and I often find new recommendations on Instagram or anywhere else I'm browsing with my intuition antennas up.

There is a quote from a famous philosopher named Schopenhauer, in which he says, "a work of art opens up a world."

Those books become a portal to a bigger, richer, more fruitful world.

And the funny thing is, with social media, "we are now truly making our own world as we go along" as Charles Hannel, the late law of attraction, transcendental philosopher said.

Following, commenting, and browsing. And we're not just leaving a wake but we're creating a rhythm and like the butterfly effect, every little thing affects everything.

Now, that "artwork opening up a world" stuff... That's interesting, right?

I mean that's the sort of shit you say to a new love and then have a romantic conversation and stare off into the distance. But it's real. Artwork does open up a world, and not just artwork.

Clothing opens up a world. Custom clothing in particular. And once you can live in that domain, you can truly build anything. Once you tune to a higher frequency as you do through the frequency of the custom cloth, you begin to live with leverage and everywhere you go and everything you do becomes effortless.

We're getting closer now.

CHAPTER 16

REAL MEN DON'T CARE BUT REAL MEN WILL NEVER TELL YOU THAT

"A wise man hears one word and understands two"

- Proverb

I've met a lot of interesting types of men in my day. I've learned from the various cultures and mentalities I've surrounded myself with, and I've noticed a thing or two. There are all kinds of men in this world. Brave, shy, strong, tired, happy, sad, exuberant, angry, distinguished, proud, joyful, serious, stern, and quiet. But no matter what man you show me, if you give me a few minutes with him... To take his measurements. To respectfully build him a powerful garment. To deliver it on time and with a smile. He will love and respect you in return. And before you know it, you will make a great friend. And not just any friend. You will make a loyal friend.

Because I don't care who you are. Rich or poor. Smart or stupid. Tall or short. We all come from somewhere and have overcome something. So, if you can proceed, without judgment, to serve, respect, and uphold the code of honesty and loyalty, then the allegiance of others will be with you. And your dreams, plans, and desires, will be for you.
That is my last certainty.
As you can see, this book has not been what you have expected. It has not been what I expected either. I opened myself up a lot here. I told you some shit I've never said in public, nevertheless in a book.

But that is what it means to write a book. In the words of the late Alan Watts, "To write a book is to say what can never be said." And that, my friends, is the beginning of an open and honest friendship.

Now, as promised, you have my word.

CHAPTER 17

THE SECRET REVEALED

"The secret is the soul of the business"

- Portuguese Proverb

Well, I never thought I would actually ever do this. You see, I've guarded my secrets over the years to respect the code. But somewhere along the way I realized that paying it forward is like sage for the soul. And to teach a business that has never been taught. To turn around and help someone else fulfill their dream of building a custom clothing business. Well, that sounds awesome. That sounds like an idea that can change the world. Of course, it doesn't sound like a high-income skill, but trust me, it is. And you can make a great living and charge a fair price and still do very well. Heck, as I hope you've seen in this book, you can have a great time doing it as well!

Guess what? Custom clothing changed my life, and

financially, it changed my world. So, if you're crazy enough to take on a business like this, I'm going to make you a limited offer. I'm not sure how long this offer will be on the table, but for now, it is.

I'm going to give you an opportunity to learn this secret trade from someone who has taken the long way in order to give you the shortcut. Now, believe me, there are no shortcuts in this business. You're going to have to study hard. But believe it or not there are some clothiers making as much or more than any standard high-paying white-collar job and working far less. It's just that no one is talking about it. Why? Take a guess. Shhhh. Not so loud. The answer is yes. You can make money. You can have fun. You can change your life's frequency by transforming how you move through the world. And yes, I've seen custom clothes get my clients paid and laid plenty of times.

And just to be clear, you can get made. Paid. And laid. By becoming a custom clothier. And you can also get paid by the benefits of building and wearing custom clothing. The question is, do you want to control the source or come to me? The choice is yours. If you liked this book and are intrigued by building an awesome wardrobe, we can help you!

If you'd like to become a custom clothier and learn the business, we can help you too!

But of course, it is going to cost you. Upfront, anyway. After that, it's going to save you and make you money by buying wholesale and selling retail!
And of course, you can write your own garments off as business expenses as the owner of a suit business. (Check with your accountant!)

So, I've paid my tuition in hard knocks and wasted time. Yours is a dollar amount that can save you time and get you started right away!

Head over to www.menswearrevolution.com today and learn how to get started!

Or as promised, you can call me. Please text first to give a heads up as I do not answer calls from unknown numbers.
Text first, and then call.
+1 (585) 703 - 4506.

Thank you!

Yours Truly,
-Nathan

The End

NOW GET READY!

To…

"DRESS ITALIAN, DRIVE GERMAN, KISS HOWEVER, AND GET PAID THE BIG BUCKS TO DO IT!"

That's right! It's your lucky day. Now it's time to learn how!

Head over to MENSWEARREVOLUTION.COM and join a select group of serious individuals embarking on a life-changing journey!

CLOTHES MORE DEALS

The Art Of FRAMING POSSIBILITY

By Nathan Minnehan

A concise exercise in understanding how to re-frame the energies in our lives by designing the clothes we wear with the energy of success. One garment at a time.

If you Engineer the Feeling of Success in Your Clothes, you can Frame Any Possibility you Desire.

This book
with its valuable message
is presented to you by

____

CLOTHES MORE DEALS

The Art Of FRAMING POSSIBILITY

"The Secret to getting what you want begins with Letting Go of and transforming WHAT is holding you back."

-NM

CLOTHES MORE DEALS
The Art Of Framing Possibility
By Nathan Minnehan

ISBN: 9781703595048

An Imprint of:

WALKNTALK
BOOKS

2336 SE Ocean Blvd #222

Stuart, Fl 34996

USA

"The Art Of FRAMING POSSIBILTY begins with what you put on each day!"

A As the saying goes the best time to plant a tree was yesterday. The next best time to do so is TODAY. The garments that we wear shape the energy we live in, either giving us access to our powerful selves or worse denying that access.

When we begin to understand that how we feel shapes how we perform in every aspect of life, it becomes ever more interesting to consider the things that shape how we feel.

It becomes all the more important to engineer those feelings so that we can put them on each day as we go out into the world to BUILD OUR DREAMS...To CLOSE MORE DEALS.

A NOTE FROM THE AUTHOR

Have you ever walked out of your house before a big meeting, and thought to yourself, "Should I really be wearing this today"?

Or how about "Why the heck did I send my best suit to the dry cleaners when I knew I would need it for today! Today is my BIG day!"

Gone are the days when any of my clothes ever made me feel "less than," or heaven for bid I was unprepared for a special occasion. Over the course of the past 24 months I have invested Tens of Thousands of dollars into my wardrobe.

Today I live in a world where when I walk out of the house, I feel on top of the world, and I have the magnetism that gives me the super power to manifest my success effortlessly everyday.

Let me give you an example of my typical day...

Walking into Starbucks or my local favorite coffee shop, I hear a voice through my headphones. It's the barista.

"WOW, I love your suit!!"

"Oh, thank you, I actually designed it."

"What! Do you have a card?"

"Sure, I'd love to give you my card."

"Hey," insert here colleague's name, "he designed his suit!"

"What... that suit is amazing! And those shoes are FIRE!"
"Well, I actually designed those too. You can design your own pair on our website."
"CARD PLEASE," says the barista's colleague...

"Gladly," I say, handing him my card.

While you may be thinking, cool story Nathan, but are those people really going to be able to buy your suits?

Great question. Actually a fellow Starbucks lover and morning regular grew to notice me. We were introduced by one of the baristas. Because of our instant connection and my style credibility in the shop, I landed him as a client. His first purchase with me was $2500. He will most likely spend five to ten thousand per year with me building his repertoire.
So, you might be thinking. That's great advertisement if you sell suits, but I'm not in the suit business Nathan, how does building my closet affect my sales?

Well, so glad you should ask.
Jim Carrey says, "The most powerful currency we have is the affect we have on others."

What would be possible if in every networking event you

attended, airplane you boarded, and PTA meeting you showed up presently for, you had with you a garment that in one simple way expressed you and your powerful life purpose objective in a way that allowed you to connect on a soulful level with a stranger within thirty to ninety seconds?

What if in your closet you had the power to cure depression, conquer your doubts, and soar like an eagle everyday?

Do you think you would CLOSE MORE DEALS?

You would certainly have the power to do so if you so chose to. Now, before we talk

garments, let's boil this all down to the nuts and bolts of transforming confidence and framing possibility with clothing.

GAME PLAN

What is the Secret to Powerfully Framing Possibility for the Obtainment of Anything You Desire?

Are you ready to live the life you have always dreamed of? To close the deals that will bring you the fruits to live your best life?

What if I told you all of this is possible so long as you are willing to let go of what is not helping you, and instead pick up the right things that will help you. The things that will bring you your success!

In this small booklet I will be giving you the tools necessary to open a new portal in your life, one that if you are willing to walk

through it, will transform everything you do into a success.

I will then show you how to craft moments that give YOU the Power, Brilliance, and Presence to CLOSE MORE DEALS in all aspects of life.

The bottom-line is if you are closing deals, then you are

winning! It doesn't matter if the deals you are closing are business deals, social contracts, or any other situation you might find yourself in. It's about having that nitro switch to go Mach 3 and turbo your way to your next level at any given moment, and doing so effortlessly!

To build that switch let's begin by establishing a few ground rules for accessing this level of effortless strength and confidence.

CLEARLY UNDERSTANDING ENERGY

What is energy and how do we harness it for our benefit?

Mood creates energy. Energy creates mood. Whoever learns how to shape mood can shape energy, and charge the environment it touches with that energy. Does that make sense?

Imagine you've won a $100,000 interior decorating package for your new house. The decorator creates a mood board to demonstrate how she can make your house look and feel when you walk in. What type of feeling would you want people to feel when they'd walk into your home? Well, if you were married with kids you'd perhaps like people to feel loved, warm, and cozy. On the other hand if you were a bachelor single and ready to mingle, you'd want women to feel turned-on when they'd walk into your home. You'd want them to feel the presence of a strong, sexy man, while still feeling intrigued to discover what's behind the curtain. You'd want them to want you.

Now, on the other hand, imagine you chose to think decor didn't matter in your house. How then would your kids and family feel when they entered if you were married with kids? And how would your sexy, hot date feel if she were to enter your home? Would either feel safe, loved, or secure? Most likely none of the above, which brings us back to our first question.

WHAT IS ENERGY?

The answer is simple. Energy is what you feel. And what you feel is what you put out into the world. Therefore, if we can create what we feel by design, then we can have more control over our outcomes. We can build the framework we live, thrive, and succeed in ALL by design. We can win in life!

MOOD

What is mood and how do we create it? Mood is the frame around the picture. Mood is what we see and feel first before we get the full picture. Mood is the vibe. Think about it. You don't say, "I got weird energy from that guy, there's a weird vibe there." You say, "I sense a weird vibe, that guy's energy must be whack!" Vibe is what we feel first, and energy is the full picture. If people don't like the vibe somewhere, they're definitely not going to stick around to test the energy.

Now, it's safe to say that mood is something we all know very well. We wake up in the morning and we sense we are in a certain mood. If you wake up alone you may feel elated to have your own space. If you wake up with the wrong person next to you, you may feel dread, and that mood may carry you into your day. So, what can we do to create the mood so that we can feel our best energy no matter who we wake up next to, and no matter what the weather looks like outside?

THE BUILDING BLOCKS OF MOOD

Everyday when we wake up, we make decisions about how we would like to appear in the world that day. "What do I FEEL like wearing today?"

That's right, in order to walk out the door you KNOW you MUST put on clothes! Unless of course you live in a nudist colony! However, I digress...

In 2019, when you walk out of the house you bring things with you. Some of the things you bring with you are things you wear, and other things are things that you carry.
What if I told you that the things you wear and carry are carrying you? That the mood they create crafts the energy you live in that day, and if done on purpose can make you powerful beyond measure.
By default, if you put on clothes that don't make you feel powerful, that depress you deep down, that make you feel less confident, then you are accepting a frame that makes you feel 'less than'. As a result, you will be putting an energy of "less than" into the world.

From the Science of Getting Rich by Wallace Wattles, we learn that the most important feelings to feel are "gratitude" and "increase". No matter what, if you can feel gratitude everyday for the life you've been given and act in such a way as to portray increase, you WILL create the future you desire!

RE-THINKING THE WAY WE WAKE UP

What would it look like if everyday you woke up and read something that DEFINITELY reminded you of where you were going in life? Then, what if you put something on that made you feel like you were already there? Then, what if you walked out the door and executed every day powerfully moving through the world with that energy? With that statement about your purpose and direction in life, you would be living on purpose with the energy of success!

Now, what would your life look like? How would people say hello to you? How would your conversations with colleagues, customers, and clients be different? Who would be leading the conversation, you or them?

How would they hear you differently? How would they see you differently? How would this shift speed up your success, and ultimately help you close more deals?

YOU ARE NOT YOUR CLOTHES BUT YOUR CLOTHES CRAFT YOUR ENERGY SO YOU CHOOSE

Many moons ago I was walking to school when a classmate joined me and I noticed his exquisite jacket, pants, and boots. Even his backpack was mint. I commented on his style. "The clothes make the man," he said. That moment stuck with me. It was something I battled, not believing that materials could create the individual. However as I got older and began building a wardrobe I noticed myself shopping on price, going to second hand, buying suits from my Turkish tailor, and shirts he "custom made", even though they weren't measured for me! I sought out suits online for cheap, and even convinced myself I looked great in my grandfather's old suits I had altered. This paradigm eventually bankrupted itself the day I met my mentor. He walked into the room and time stopped. His energy, smile, and presence were larger than life. He was a sartorial savant, and I was intrigued. When I found out the price of his jacket I nearly fell over. I had no idea things could be so expensive. He quickly educated me.

"If you want to close real deals, and do real business, you have to dress with the correct materials."

"Clothes are not expensive, clothes create the close and that's profit! It's the other way around!"

We walked to his store and I tried on my first investment piece. I had never felt that feeling. That power. That material. Suddenly I looked at everything else I was wearing and soon it all felt like a leaky ship. Feeling the power of that garment revealed energy gaps in the clothes I was already wearing. The next few years were massively transformative. I looked at my closet and realized that the guy getting dressed everyday was sabotaging my real success. I looked in the mirror and realized something had to change. I began to look forward to crafting more garments. I sorted my clothing into two groups. I realized I had been buying clothing that was interesting, however there was little to no continuity between the garments. I thought I had built a wardrobe, when really I had collected a closet that resembled a compost of garments I hardly wore, and yet I wondered why I wasn't getting the results I wanted in my life.

CREATE AND DESTROY

One of my most influential life mentors, Dr. Gene Landrum, the creator and founder of Chuck E. Cheese, once said "you have to be willing to intentionally destroy yourself in order to powerfully re-create yourself." What he meant by this was that you have to be willing to let go in order to receive. If you make space for the new you can receive the new you. If you're stubborn and unwilling to admit that the things you are doing are not working, then how can you change them? The most powerful tool we have is change, and yet the whole world resists it. What would it take for this message to really sink in? What would it take for you to make the change you know you desperately need to make in your life?

THE EXPERIMENT

Consider Donating All of your Clothes

How much of your closet do you really wear? Five to ten shirts? Five to ten suits? A few casual slacks? Ten to fifteen pair of underwear, and twenty socks and plain white or black tees? A couple of dress shoes? One or two pair of sneakers?

What would your life look like if the clothes you wore made you feel, embody, and attract your success everyday? What if you could rid your life of all of your previous inhibitions? What if you could reconstruct the real, powerful you through clothing that told the story about your commitment to success, and your life purpose? What if the vibration of your unique vision of success was designed into your clothing like a chip into a computer to run the program of success everyday?

Then what would be possible?

EFFORTLESSLY MANIFESTING YOUR SUCCES

WHAT IS YOUR Narrative and what does it have to do with your success?

"The Story You're Telling Yourself and The World Around You Without Saying a Word." - Narrative

When you wake up in the morning and get dressed, you put on stories. Those stories then walk out the door with you and speak singlehandedly. The way those clothes are making you feel is either putting out a contagious vibe of success, or detracting from success by making you subconscious and feel "less than".

What is it then costing you not to look and feel your best everyday? How is your half-baked wardrobe serving your self-conscious need to sabotage yourself for fear that you might outshine or offend others along the way?

What would it take to give yourself permission to take back your right to live fully empowered, and make a real investment in yourself?

ACCESSING POSSIBILITY THROUGH CLOTHING

If you're still reading this, then you're most likely beginning to see the point. You are beginning to realize that how you feel is very important. How you feel affects how you perform, and how others see you. What if we were to flip the script? Instead of asking why someone would invest in their wardrobe, and spend real money on clothing, ask instead, why wouldn't someone powerfully moving in the direction of their success, invest in themselves by investing in their clothing? Which brings us to the next point.

PERSONAL BRAND —> BUILD IT OR KILL IT!

In the community of people you operate in, both online and in person, you have a certain type of perception you have crafted about yourself. People either talk about you or they don't. They either love you, hate you, or Worse, Don't Even Notice you!

What is your personal brand, and how do you create it?

Your personal brand begins with that energy you bring into the world. The way you make others feel! It's what you do, how you do it, and what you're known for. When it comes to clothing and building a wardrobe, I have successfully helped powerful people around the globe enhance their personal brands by crafting garments for them that tell stories that instantly confer their value, influence, and brilliance on the world around them.

From Dr. Greg Reid, author of 65 books and counting, to Kajabi co-founder, Travis Rosser, to the creator of the Make A Wish foundation, Frank Shankwitz, to Ron Klein, the inventor of the magnetic strip on the credit card, and several other famous people living their best lives, I have had the pleasure of helping all of them tell powerful stories with their garments.

When a jacket, suit, shirt, or coat you are wearing has been designed for you it carries with it an energy more powerful than the most expensive GUCCI or Prada piece off the rack.

PEOPLE WILL NOTICE AND OFTEN ASK.

EXAMPLE 1 [Exercising the "CLOSE" / CLOTHES]

"Wow that's a beautiful jacket, I love the stitching."

ANSWER:
"Oh thank you, this is my clarity jacket. The blue stitching is one of my mantras for success and clarity in everything I do."

"Really? Tell me more about that, what do you do?"
"Well, I help real people find real value in their next real estate purchase."
"Wow, that's powerful, my husband and I were just thinking about buying an investment property here in the Fort Lauderdale area. Our daughters just moved down here for college."

"Oh really," he says opening his jacket. "I keep my kids right here with me everyday. They're the motivation behind everything I do, and so I have photos of them in the lining of all of my suits and jackets."

"GET OUT OF HERE!" "Wow, that is so powerful. My husband and I are definitely going to call you!"

"Here, would you mind punching in your best contact information? I'll send you a text with my info."

"Oh perfect, yes, that's easy. Great, well thank you so much! My husband and I will most definitely be in touch!"

"Thank you miss. I will send you my information now."

"Okay great, take care!"

Observations

Did you notice how the man's jacket instantly gave him control in the conversation? How everything they were talking about went directly back to what he was wearing, almost like flaps in a pinball machine? He kept wracking up the points, over and over until she reached a point of certainty that she will definitely reach out. Then, the trained "closer," not wanting to leave anything up to chance made the smartest next move, and gave her his phone with an open contact allowing her to easily give him the best contact information. With all of the balls now in his court, it's up to him to score.

PERSONAL BRAND RESIDUALS

What Other People Say about You Is a Residual you Can create through the Power of Your Personal Brand!

The other day I received a phone call.

"Hello, this is Nathan."

"Yes, Nathan, this is Mark."

"Hi Mark, how can I help you?"

"Well, I need help with my website and Jackie told me she knows the only guy to work with and gave me your information. I looked you up online, saw your suits and instantly I knew you were the guy!"

"Well, thank you Mark. What kind of project, timeline, and budget are we working with here?"

"I have six hundred shoes to move before Christmas. I need a new e-commerce store in two weeks, and I want to pump Instagram with ads to sell out all of my shoes!"

"Excellent! You're talking to the guy who can make that happen. What do you say I take a look at your product, and get you a quote in forty-eight hours and we'll move forward then? Does that sound good?"

"Yes! I just love your style, and professionalism, and I know you're the guy for the job!"

"Excellent, thank you Mark. I will call you Thursday at this same time. Does that work for you?"
"Yes that's perfect, thank you Nathan!"
"It's my pleasure Mark. I look forward to positioning your brand for success!"

"Okay, talk soon."

"Bye now."

How likely do you think Mark is to buy from Nathan? Why was Mark referred to Nathan? What did Nathan do to become the guy who owns a suit company, yet has created a personal brand that establishes trust with perfect strangers to do business with him on a completely different vertical?

Simple Answer: He invested in himself and spent real time, real money, and real energy building his wardrobe and online image.

Longer Answer:

Nathan took the advice of Dr. Gene Landrum and intentionally destroyed himself to powerfully re-create himself. He donated/ gifted nearly all most of his clothes and rebuilt his wardrobe one intentional garment at a time. He established a mantra that frames every garment he wears and therefore sets the mood of success so that he feels the energy of success everyday, everywhere he goes. Anything in his closet that made him feel "less than" he donated or gifted. He designed clothing that told stories to himself and others that established confidence and trust in himself and his abilities.

What else did he do to earn that reputation?

He moved. He gave up the old apartment that was holding him back. He moved into a new energy by crafting a new frame. He donated his clothes, built every new garment by design, and let go of a house and a city that no longer defined him. He changed his energy, and therefore changed his life. He examined all of the ways he was appearing online and reached his next level of success by intentionally destroying to powerfully recreate himself. He hired photographers and branding gurus to help him reach his next level, and vowed to never be complacent.

CLOSING THOUGHTS

If you're not growing you're shrinking. If you're not living, you're dying.

"An old suit carries with it old inhibitions, a new suit carries with it a blank canvas, and the possibility of a new powerful version of oneself" -Prentice Mulford, Thoughts are Things

Put simply, if any of the garments in your closet remind you of your failures or previous inhibited states, then they need to go.

It's time to do some math and decide how much you can afford to spend on

your wardrobe yearly, then double that figure. "Double it?" Yes, "double it."

Garments created just for you as illustrated in the previous stories will not cost you money. They will MAKE YOU MONEY. They will help you CLOSE MORE DEALS.

TAKE ACTION

To find out more about how you can begin to CLOSE MORE DEALS, reach out to one of Nathan's team members and schedule your first truly bespoke success clothing consultation with the man writing this text!

IF you want success, then you must engineer it. Begin first by engineering the mindset, setting the mood, tone, vibe, and energy of success with garments that convert more situations in your life into the success you desire. The success that gives you the WIN!

Big Murphy's
OTHING
BESPOKE SUITS
AND CUSTOM MENSWEAR
BigMurphys.com

Women's Clothing
Lady Cuyler
women's clothing
www.ladycuyler.com

Give CLOTHES MORE DEALS to your Friends

Visit www.nathan.life to find the direct link
to buy CLOTHES MORE DEALS on Amazon.
For packs of 100 you can purchase them
directly from us via:
www.nathan.life

GC
TECH
Every once in a while a product comes along that you have no idea how you lived without before. That is the experience of GCTECH shoe covers. They absolutely redline on all fronts. Style, comfort, performance, practicality. You can literally bet you'll be covered rain, snow, or shine. And you won't believe the compliments I get. Hands down, what every sophisticated gentleman didn't know they needed, and soon will never want to live without!
Nathan Minnehan
-Founder of Big Murphy's
ORDER ONLINE AT:
www.gctechdesign.com &
www.bigmurphys.com

A MASTERCLASS SERIES

"Read this book and be inspired to find your voice, gain confidence and get more joy out of life."
— Susan Berkley, signature voice of citi

SPEAK
FOR YOURSELF

7 POWERFUL WAYS TO
SPEAK UP
SHUT UP AND
SHOW UP

JERRY LOBOZZO

SPEAKFORYOURSELFMASTERCLASS.COM

Oh, by the way, do yourself a favor, and get this book!

www.ingramcontent.com/pod-product-compliance
Lightning Source LLC
LaVergne TN
LVHW050649100826
845148LV00011B/2041
9798950444029